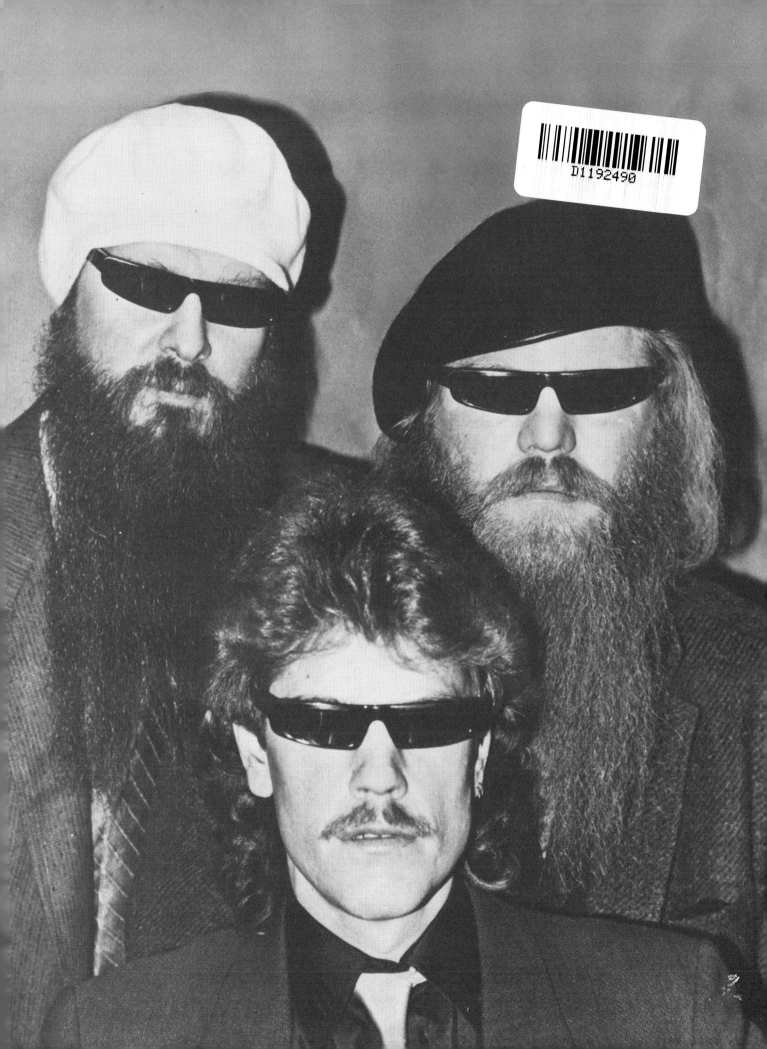

A ROLLING STONE PRESS BOOK

BAD AND WORLDWIDE

Z Z T O P

by
Deborah Frost

Photographs by Bob Alford

COLLIER BOOKS / MACMILLAN PUBLISHING COMPANY
New York

Macmillan Publishing Company
866 Third Avenue, New York, N.Y. 10022
Collier Macmillan Canada, Inc.

Library of Congress Cataloging in Publication Data
Frost, Deborah.
    ZZ Top: bad and worldwide.
    "A Rolling Stone Press book."
    1. ZZ Top (Musical group) 2. Rock musicians—
United States—Biography. I. Title.
ML421.Z98F7 1985   784.5′4′00922 [B]   85-7797
ISBN 0-02-002950-0

Macmillan books are available at special discounts
for bulk purchases for sales promotions, premiums,
fund-raising, or educational use. For details, contact:
    Special Sales Director
    Macmillan Publishing Company
    866 Third Avenue
    New York, N.Y. 10022

10 9 8 7 6 5 4 3 2 1

Printed in the United States of America

CONTENTS

PROLOGUE
9

CHAPTER 1
Billy
13

CHAPTER 2
The Mangy Mutts,
the Blue Flames and
Other Tall Tales
16

CHAPTER 3
The Moving
Sidewalks...
Moving
26

CHAPTER 4
ZZ's
Beginnings
31

CHAPTER 5
Dusty
37

CHAPTER 6
Frank
Beard
40

CHAPTER 7
Dusty, Frank
& Billy
44

CHAPTER 8
The
Records
49

CHAPTER 9
The Texas
Tour
63

CHAPTER 10
The Long
Vacation
70

CHAPTER 11
The
Comeback
77

CHAPTER 12
El Loco
90

CHAPTER 13
The Big Daddy/
Eliminator
96

DISCOGRAPHY AND
VIDEOGRAPHY
120

FOR JUDITH, DAVID, JONATHAN & SARA

You didn't have to...but you did & you did & I THANK YOU:

Jay Lovinger, my great editor at *People* who let me go out and get this in the first place. David McGee, my editor at the *Record*, whose sensitive eye for a story has made mine (including the *Record*'s version of this one) so much better and whose sympathetic ear has gotten me through so many of the darker days. David Hirshey—and Fred Schruers—for introducing me to Jay Lovinger. Robert Christgau, for his advice, many insights and his agent. Albert Bouchard and Paul Nelson for keeping me running. Tom DeFlora, for being a legend and keeping me pumped. Albert Poland, for being The Peaches—toujours. To Trix Rosen, for keeping me... encouraged. Kit Rachlis, for locking me in the room long ago. Kurt Loder, for sharing his notes. William Lee Frost & co. for the fan club. To Eva Frost, for her humor. Rob Falk, David Godbey, Madeleine le Roux. Miriam Klipper. Thanks (and oinks) to Jay, Geraldine, Lauren and Benjamin Warner. Thanks, Jeffrey Ferry, for the good time. And Jimmy Mack McInerney for the good phone and "negative innuendos." To my agent, Robert Cornfield, for service above and beyond... Thank you to everyone at Rolling Stone Press for your help and your patience—Dulcy Israel, Carrie Schneider, Mary Astadourian, Ilene Cherna, Jonathan Wells, and especially my editor, Tim McGinnis. Thank you to Tim Newman and everyone from Tanglewood and Texas for their time and their tales. And thank you to Billy Gibbons, Dusty Hill and Frank Beard for fiiiine evenings in Des Moines, Biloxi, New Orleans and Houston and giving us all their lovin' on so many hot platters.

MORNING in Santa Monica: The sky is blue and the ocean is freezing. Somewhere on that promising horizon, above the shimmer of white and silver sand, Linda Ronstadt is slipping out of her teddie. Around the corner at Olympic and Pico, Arnold Schwarzenegger contemplates a couple pounds of chopped sirloin. Valley kids duded up like Motley Ratts are cranking their ghetto blasters and trying to stop traffic. In other words, it is a long way from Texas. But for a moment, as he surveys the scene beneath the expansive terrace of his art deco hotel suite, Texas is on Tim Newman's mind.

Newman spent his Hollywood youth in the shadow of his famous, film-scoring father. He spent his adulthood (despite a solid rep in advertising as a director of comedy and dialogue commercials for products forgotten as soon as the film's in the can) as "Randy Newman's cousin." If it wasn't for Texas Newman might not be en route to a meeting with a studio honcho. If it were not for Tim Newman, who did a great dialogue and comedy number on their product, four rock and roll cowboys might still be trying to accomplish what they'd been shooting toward for 15 years. Which cowboys? Three are

Rub-a-dub-dub...three men on a hog.

seen onstage, known publicly and collectively as ZZ Top. One stays back at the ranch/office, making the whole thing spin. Not only do they bring a bit of Texas to the world but they also satisfy ambitions and egos as large as the Lone Star state.

In 1976, ZZ Top toured with a buffalo, a longhorn steer, four buzzards, cacti and rattlesnakes. Despite ASPCA approval (and Society members were always snooping) and air-conditioned trailers, the rattlesnakes, which occupied a plastic dome in the Brownsville section of the Texas-shaped stage couldn't handle the vibrations of one of the most outrageous concepts in rock. They died along the trail.

In 1979, after a three-year lay-off that freed ZZ Top from their London Records contract and allowed them to sign with Warner, they released *Deguello*, which means "Spare no quarter" in Spanish. *Deguello* was the order that brought down the Alamo. That was always the idea behind ZZ's live show. But no matter what kind of attack they launched (or how many innocents were lost), the band could get arrested for driving while blind, and that was about it. In 1976, ZZ Top still wasn't bad or worldwide.

Over the course of eight albums (their first came in 1970) ZZ Top had a couple of bar band classics —"Tush" and "La Grange"—and a few modest FM songs, like "Cheap Sunglasses," to their credit. The band holds a perennial appeal as a live attraction to beer-drinkers and hell-raisers. And the bruising, funky picking of Billy Gibbons attracts guitar worshippers. But as Rodney Dangerfield might say, they get no respect.

To their mortification, Dusty Hill and Billy Gibbons were once singled out by Rodney during his Las Vegas act. Spotting the two balding men in the front row, Dangerfield asked, "What is this, some new cult with haircuts with a hole in the middle?"

They were still a boogie band—one that had graduated from bars to arenas—but a boogie band nonetheless. But with the release of their ninth album, *Eliminator*, in 1983, these hairy, unlikely rock heroes had become a pop phenomenon.

This had something to do with the discoveries of a young preproduction engineer whose contributions, like those of many associated with the band over the years, were never acknowledged. This engineer suggested the band rev up their rhythm to 120 beats per minute, which, according to his computer studies, is the natural human dance speed. This let people do what they'd never been able to do to a ZZ Top record before, namely dance.

"Musicians don't dance," explained the engineer. "They look down from the bandstand and the people on the floor dancing look like animals to them. It does something funny to their minds." The effect was not unlike putting a new, supercharged engine in an old car and making it run better than ever.

But the real evolution of ZZ Top from comfortable but inefficient bluesmobile to modern speedster would not have been possible without the emergence of MTV. Tim Newman, knew how to use this new rock marketing medium to maximum advantage. Newman created the girls and keychains scenario that showed Billy Gib-

bons, Dusty Hill and Frank Beard in a lovable, humorous light. It was, perhaps more than any other factor, responsible for their ultimate break. For Newman, it was simply another gig.

Newman leaned back on his well-stuffed art deco couch. The studio honcho was waiting. He ran his hand through his salt-and-pepper hair and tried to explain his part in the ZZ Top story.

When Jo Bergman of Warner Brothers Records first broached the subject of a video, his ZZ awareness was about as high as the next guy's. Sure, he'd heard of them. He'd even heard their music—if pressed, he could reach into the depths of his consciousness and come up humming a few bars of "Tush." But who were they? What were they? Like the rest of the world, until Newman took a camera and a crew out to a desert gas station to film the band, he didn't really know, either.

"Okay, they said, here's the assignment," he explained. "Here's the album. On this album there is this hot rod. If you could work in the car, that would be good." The rest is a little piece of rock & roll history.

Would you buy a used roadster from these men?

CHAPTER I

BILLY

IF subsequent performances have been any indication, William Frederick Todd Gibbons probably entered this world on Dec. 12, 1949 screaming "Have mercy!"

Billy Gibbons was *always* different. Just about anyone who knew him as a boy in Tanglewood, "the second nicest neighborhood in Houston," will tell you so. (River Oaks is first). Gibbons' father was a little different, too. Maybe that explains it.

Fred Gibbons was a Yankee, a New Yorker who was 42 when his only son was born. He'd moved to Texas, where his first wife's family owned a chain of movie theatres. He had hoped the climate would benefit his wife's failing health. Unfortunately, she died (leaving a daughter, Billy's half-sister, now in her fifties, who lives in Houston). Although he did a stint playing organ in one of his in-laws' Iris theatres, by the time he married Billy's mother, a one-time model, Fred Gibbons had established himself as *the* Houston society bandleader. He also conducted the Houston Philharmonic, arranged music for films in Hollywood and for big bands in Las Vegas. The long car trips the family took to accompany Fred gave Billy his first taste of the road and turned him into what he described as a "lover of the Southwest."

For younger sister Pam, the highlight of one Vegas family junket was a poolside encounter with Humphrey Bogart. For Billy, it was several backstage encounters with pasties and G-strings. Later, he compared his father's career to his own: "When my dad would play, people'd order an old-fashioned. To a ZZ show, they bring a fifth."

Fred Gibbons died while Billy was playing in Las Vegas in 1981. The father contracted a staph infection while having his teeth cleaned at the dentist—one of those one-in-a-million flukes. Billy had visited him only a few days before, and asked his father to give him some kind of sign. His father looked at him and said, "You know what to do."

Unlike the fathers of Billy's friends, Fred Gibbons worked at night and was home during the day, which enabled him to develop an unusual relationship with his son. Many of Billy's bands—from the Saints to early ZZ Top—rehearsed at his house. They got to know Gibbons, Sr. Their interaction usually took the form of an irate Fred, roused by a bum note, screaming something to the effect of "That

Billy bites down hard on a custom Erlewine Doubleneck.

was supposed to be a C sharp, you ninny!" before returning to his sheet music. Fred would often read sheet music for entertainment, the way most people read a magazine.

"My Dad and I were great buddies," recalls Billy. "He was so much older than most Dads. He had that edge. Plus, he was a musician, and after I started playing, that was a great point to relate to."

Billy started playing in 1963, when he discovered a Gibson Melody Marker and a little Fender Champ amp beneath the Christmas tree. Although there's no doubt from whom Billy inherited his musical gifts (everyone recalls Fred Gibbons as a pianist extraordinaire), his taste was influenced by the family maid. Or, to be precise, by Little Stella, daughter of family maid, Big Stella.

Billy started pestering his father for a guitar when he first saw Elvis on TV. But when Little Stella took him and Pam to see Little Richard (who, like other great R&B artists performed frequently in Houston), Gibbons went straight to Good Golly heaven.

"That's one reason there's a lot of blues influences," he explained 20 years later, as ZZ Top wound up their eight-month *Eliminator* tour in Biloxi. "Cause my dad certainly wasn't doin' gut-bucket blues. But Little Stella was always buying the records and that's what we were listening to. All the Little Richard stuff, Larry Williams' 'Short Fat Fanny,' Jimmy Reed, T-Bone Walker, B. B. King, the usual lineup of R&B stars."

So many of his local contemporaries went on to form bands that had regional followings and recorded regional hits, in fact, that

the neighborhood became known as "the Tanglewood Rock Factory." Billy's fascination with R&B set him apart from his schoolmates. Fever Tree rhythm guitarist Don Lampton, who graduated from Lee High School a year ahead of Billy (who got out in 1967) remembers that while his friends were "running around listening to the Yardbirds, and playing "We Gotta Get Out of This Place' by Eric Burdon and the Animals, Billy was into black music."

Billy got his blues from the source instead of second-hand, from England. But that wasn't the only thing that made him different. While other boys were pursuing another favorite hobby, making model cars of Jaguar XKEs, Billy was gluing together ancient Fords. As Don Lampton explains,

"Texas is not quite the Wild West. But in the school systems, and in the way we grew up down here, certain things were considered important. If you were to participate in a school band or choir, you were a sissy. If you played football or basketball, track or baseball—especially football—you could be the stud of the school. Men were not pushed toward entertainment. So somebody that could perform, whether it was playing the guitar or singing, was really a rarity. You had to have balls to get up there and do it, because of all the criticism. My dad didn't want me to play in bands. Singing and playing guitars, they're for sissies. But Billy, he never had any inhibitions at all. If the place was completely packed, he would act the same as if there were two people in the room. I don't know too many people that at 14 can fall down on their knees in front of a bunch of other kids and do James Brown's 'Please, Please, Please.' and pull it off,'' That's what made him different.

Billy Gibbons was not only getting down James Brown's "huhs" and Howlin' Wolf howls, he was also working up a file of fat, satisfaction-guaranteed guitar licks. He was perfecting the art of the practical joke. In Texas, where spinning yarns is a state pastime, Billy's schoolboy-showman tales had to be taller than anyone else's. He would do anything to put anybody on. He might spend an afternoon pretending he was just off the plane from London. Or he might walk around for an entire weekend talking like Blind Lemon Jefferson. Often he'd take a story a friend had told him and turn it inside out, as if he'd been there or it had happened to him. Most people chalked it up to his being a little guy. He was just the kind of kid you'd let tag along only because he was so damn insistent. The kid who was always picked last for the team. But the kind of kid who'd do anything, absolutely anything, for attention. The kid who, even while sitting there waiting and waiting, was going to make sure you couldn't ignore him. And for awhile, everybody thought it was a real hoot.

"Down on your knees, please, please, please."

THE MANGY MUTTS, THE BLUE FLAMES AND OTHER TALL TALES

BILLY Gibbons likes to reminesce about his days with the Mangy Mutts. These days, depending on the weather or one of his whims, Billy will tell people he launched his career on either a record label called "Mangy Mutt Records" or as a guitar player in a band of the same name. He's even taken to passing around singles with "Mangy Mutt" right there on the label. And then there's Billy G. and his Ten Blue Flames, the "very loose R & B horn band" Billy likes to tell interviewers about now. Both the Mangy Mutts and the Flames were so loose they never existed, except in Billy Gibbons' imagination. Even if he did go to the trouble of having Mutts records pressed recently or gotten a photo lab to paste together an old snapshot of a little Billy with another bunch of old, black "Flames." Presto, it's instant history, evidence to back up stories that, even in Texas, might be described "loco."

Billy started banging around in the garage with a loose outfit called the Saints, but his first real, steadily gigging band was the Coachmen. They were named after the Coachman Inn, a teen club operated by Richard and Steve Ames, local

promoters, producers and managers who, like many in Houston, kept one foot in their oil wells and the other in rock'n'roll.

Dan Mitchell was Billy Gibbons' best friend and drummer through high school, the Coachmen, the Moving Sidewalks and ZZ Top. He was fired and replaced by Frank Beard. Mitchell can't understand what had motivated Gibbons' casual reinterpretation of their mutual past.

"I've always written it off as publicity," he says. "But it got to a point where it hurt a lot of people's feelings. The people who deserve credit shouldn't be made fun of, because they deserve recognition."

Back in 1966 the Coachmen's notion of recognition meant a booking for the high school prom. But then they recorded "99th Floor" their homage to the 13th-Floor Elevators. Billy scribbled it one afternoon in math class. Pursuing his new infatuation all the way, he converted the Coachmen's name and format from soul to the psychedelic Moving Sidewalks. The Sidewalks became regional stars.

As Dan Mitchell remembers, "We played every nightclub in Texas and Louisiana on a regular

What is under this man's hat? Billy on one of his frequent trips to Mexico. Despite the sign, Billy says NASA turned down his request that ZZ Top be the first band to play the space shuttle. The trio, despite all their peculiarities, does not qualify as a "scientific experiment."

basis for four or five nights a week. '99th Floor' was a good-sized single in Texas. It was number one in Houston for five weeks. Scepter/Wand tried to make it a national hit. It ended up getting airplay in several Southern cities, but it was successful for us in Texas. So we got a lot of opportunity. We were making pretty good money. We played a lot of private parties and things from anywhere from $400 up. Normally, at the end, we were getting anywhere from $800 to $1,000, which was pretty good money in 1968 for four kids just out of high school."

Despite his local stardom and relative riches, Billy's mother wouldn't let him grow his hair. He lived at home well after high school—friends say he didn't get his own place until 1975. His mother wasn't too thrilled abut his career at first, either. Billy's father, as a professional musician, was far more sympathetic., although he did wish Billy would find colleagues who knew more than three chords. One day, Fred heard the inspired riffing of a technically accomplished keyboard player above the usual jam session cacophony. He got so excited he ran out to the garage in his pajamas.

But Billy's mother, like many of the Tanglewood parents, had to be convinced that the noise and the long hair would somehow pay off. Her interests ran more to politics than pop, and she worked on the campaigns of John F. Kennedy and Lyndon Johnson. Billy says that he and sister Pam took the personally autographed photo Johnson gave their mother and turned it into a dart board—just what any self-respecting hippie would do. Billy

claims his mother's political ties with LBJ were such that the President would come to their house, and their street would be cordoned off by the Secret Service. She didn't want her visitors running into her son's friends. One Tanglewood Factory rocker remembers stopping by Billy's to pick up a piece of equipment for a gig, and being told by Mrs. Gibbons to hurry up and leave. She was expecting company, and didn't want her guest's appetites ruined by the sight of this unsavory character, whose bangs might have just reached his eyebrows.

If Billy had to behave at home, onstage he was a wild man. Long before Kiss and Mötley Crüe started playing with matches, Billy took Arthur Brown's "Fire" literally. He'd torch the stage. The Moving Sidewalks also used strobe lights and explosives for dramatic—and in one case, near tragic—results. Dan Mitchell was fooling around with some stage props when someone got careless with a cigarette. No one is sure what happened, but the big bang nearly cost Mitchell one side of his face. Alvin Lee and Leo Lyons of Ten Years After, with whom the Sidewalks were sharing a bill, rushed him to the hospital. The attendants shared Mrs. Gibbons' reaction to long hair. They wanted him to leave.

In Texas, in 1969, a Tanglewood rocker recalled, "Having long hair was a strong statement."

Playing guitars made of toilet seats or fur-covered instruments that spun around like some amusement-park attraction may also be a statement. The fur-covered (or, as Billy calls them, the Billy G. Ultra-Bush models) were originally con-

During the band's lay off, even the guitars grew beards. The Ultra-Bush guitar from Billy's famed collection.

On the beach at Malibu: the boys and their baby.

cocted for the Sidewalks' appearance with the Doors in Houston. They had to do something memorable, or the audience might forget the opening act as soon as the headliner unzipped his fly. The Sidewalks were apparently memorable enough to garner one of the first standing ovations in Houston rock-concert history.

The Ultra Bushes recently made a comeback. They're probably familiar to anyone who's seen ZZ Top's "Legs" video. Dan Mitchell can't figure that out either. New instruments were ordered by Billy and custom-built for "Legs" by Don Summers, the Sidewalks' bass player now trying to establish himself as a guitarmaker. In at least one recent interview, Gibbons said he couldn't remember his former bassist's name or what he'd been up to. It seemed like a strange joke to play on an old friend, especially

to a friend would could use the mention and career boost.

Nobody has yet figured out how to help Gibbons manufacture his ultimate spoof: a playable live-goldfish-in-a-plexiglass fishbowl guitar. From the beginning Billy was dreaming up wild guitars. As a young teenager he painted and customized a red pin-striped one with the same basic design as the $50,000 hot rod he was able to afford over 20 years later. Gibbons has had plenty of guitars. Among aficionados, he may be almost as famous for his crazy guitar collection as for his playing. He owns many beautiful vintage instruments, and some novelty items as well: the toilet seat guitar, Ultra Bushes, another made from Model T parts, the Chiquita miniature travel guitar, and a Gibson shaped like the state of Texas. On the *Eliminator* tour, he and Dusty played

Billy to Dusty: "Eat my exhaust."

toy-sized car-shaped guitars. The volume and tone controls were in the spinning hubcaps. Exhaust shot from the tailpipes at the end of the opening number. Unfortunately, it also put a weird buzz through the P. A., so they had to cool their jets.

As wild as some of Gibbons' guitars are, the stories he often tells about them are even wilder.

Like Pearly Gates, the primo 1959 sunburst Les Paul largely responsible for Gibbons' distinctive aural patina. Pearly gave him the original growl that makes ZZ Top come off like (as he told Kurt Loder in Rolling Stone) "four flat tires on a muddy road." Pearly is too valuable to make public appearances so Billy has since spent many hours and many dollars trying to duplicate Pearly's unique qualities with his other guitars. Gibbons says that the other ingredients for his secret sound recipe include ZZ Top's private-label Rio Grande amplifiers (despite the dice where control knobs would be, they're really Marshalls with "Rio Grande" faceplates), using a peso instead of a pick for that international flavor (although he often uses a conventional pick in concert, and carries a peso in a velvet pouch for show) and guitar strings he claims are made from melted auto bumpers. Through his fan club, he even markets these strings (according to the guy who turned him on to the buy-in-bulk deal years ago, he gets them for 90¢ a set from La Bella in Long Island). But Pearly Gates is so special, she's the cover girl on ZZ Top's first album. When Billy recorded a song with another guitar, he titled it "Apologies to Pearly." And yet, her origins remain mysterious.

The improbable story Billy tells about Pearly involves a girlfriend who drove a 1930s Packard (according to his friends, the Packard is as tangible as Billy G's Blue Flames) to L.A. to audition for a movie. Once there, she sold the car and sent him $450. Miracle of miracles, the money arrived the same day he'd found an incredible instrument for that price under some farmer's bed out in the country.

According to several of Billy's Tanglewood cronies, it wasn't unusual to find guitars in such places. That part of the tale is entirely plausible. During the era of Bob Wills, the singing cowboy, every other cowboy in Texas bought a guitar. Most of the instruments ended up under beds or in attics.

Several of Billy's friends made a comfortable living going out and finding them. (They didn't even wait for want ads—they often worked from a list of old customer receipts and warranties from local music stores.) Especially in the late 1960s and early 1970s when Fender had been sold to CBS and few good electric guitars were being made, these instruments were especially desirable. Finding a precious Pearly would be something like coming across a Stradivarius. Pearly's real owner lived in Houston and was no farmer. He wouldn't part with her for anything, certainly not for the $1,000 cash or the choice of other expensive guitars one of the Tanglewood entrepreneurs offered him.

But the man's young son didn't have the same sentimental attachment to Pearly. And whatever deal did go down, the result was that Billy got the guitar. Perhaps the kid got a beating. But the couple of hundred dollars he also got was probably more money than he'd ever seen before.

But perhaps the most famous guitar and the most famous guitar story associated with Billy Gibbons is the story of the pink Hendrix guitar. When the Moving Sidewalks toured with Jimi Hendrix, Hendrix was so impressed with Gibbons that he presented Billy with a pink Fender Stratocaster. It's been repeated so often and in so many places that no one, maybe even Billy himself these days, would believe it's not true. The story is often accompanied, as it was in the 1984 story in *Rolling Stone* by a photograph of Hendrix, the "Hendrix guitar" and the Moving Sidewalks.

It is a fact that the Moving Sidewalks did encounter Jimi Hendrix. Riding high with the success of "99th Floor," the Sidewalks played four shows (two in Houston, one in both Dallas and San Antonio) as part of a show headlined by Jimi Hendrix. Over the years, these four shows have turned into a big tour. The pink guitar has been used to forge a link between great guitarist Jimi and his young apostle Billy in Texas.

According to Dan Mitchell, the Sidewalks also ran into Hendrix in a hotel lobby later in their career. They said hello and recalled their bill together, and that was about the extent of the relationship. He can't remember where that happened, but it probably wasn't San Antonio. Don Lampton was in

charge of making hotel arrangements for Hendrix in Texas. He recalls that they couldn't get Hendrix a reservation in town. He wasn't only black, he was rock 'n' roll. The only place that would give him a bed was a motel out on Interstate 35.

According to those backstage at the Sidewalks-Hendrix shows (the Sidewalks were one of three acts preceding the headliner) Hendrix was impressed with Gibbons' playing. If you listen to the Sidewalks' LP, you can understand Hendrix' enthusiasm. Much of what Billy was doing at that time was an imitation of Jimi. Hendrix wasn't as impressed with the other local guitar stars who appeared on the bills: Jimmy Vaughan (Stevie Ray's big brother, now of the Thunderbirds, then of the Chessmen, a legendary Dallas outfit) and the guitarists with the fanatics.

Hendrix did try to trade a guitar with the guitarist Jon Pereles who played with Neil Ford and the Fanatics, a rival band of the Sidewalks. Hendrix wanted to swap a 12-string for a Pereles Stratocaster. The deal didn't come off. Hendrix gave a couple of items away—a pendant he wore on the cover of Jimi Hendrix' *Smash Hits*, to Richard Ames, who promoted the

The Moving Sidewalks pose with the Voodoo Chile: (left to right), Tom Moore, Jimi Hendrix, Don Summers, Billy Gibbons and Dan Mitchell.

shows with his brother Steve, and a guitar strap to Annette Cope, the production company's secretary.

One local musician speculates Billy saw Hendrix try to trade with Perelen and later changed the point of view. Maybe the Hendrix guitar story started when Gibbons was sitting in the studio and wanted a variation on the Pearly Gates/Les Paul sound he became well-known for early in his career. Like almost everyone else who's reached for a Stratocaster in a similar situation, he may have said to his roadie, "No, the Les Paul isn't right for this track. I need that Hendrix sound here. Get me a Hendrix guitar." The name stuck, a myth was born.

A Tanglewood friend remembers. "There were about 15 of us who ran around together. We were all either in bands or involved with bands. We hung out at the Ames' home, at the swimming pool. We'd play pool inside, drink Coca-Colas and eat their delicatessen food all day long. It was a country club for us. If Hendrix had given Billy a pink Strat then, *one* of us would've found out about it."

As for the famous photo of Hendrix holding a guitar and posing with a young, barely bearded Gibbons and the other Sidewalks, it was a black and white polaroid snapped by a roadie. The guitar held by Hendrix wasn't his own, and it wasn't even pink.

Kurt Linhof, who played bass with The Children knows about the pink guitar's origin. It was one of three Stratocasters he and Billy painted in the garage. He even remembers the name of the paint: 1956 Ford Pink. He still has one of them at home in Denver.

The Hendrix story doesn't stop

there. The rumor was refueled when ZZ Top's Houston warehouse was burglarized in 1979 and Gibbons declared his prized pink "Hendrix" guitar among the missing. He found former FeverTree lead guitarist Michael Knust playing it in Remington's, a Houston club. Knust says he bought it for $200 from a lawyer who'd gotten it in lieu of a client's fee. Billy walked into Remington's with two huge men in suits and offered Knust $250. Knust thought at first Gibbons was trying to sign him to his record label or management company, until Billy pulled out photos of the guitar. Gibbons made a big, almost insulting to-do about it, telling him he was making $50 on the deal. Knust called him a few days later and said, half in jest, that he didn't mind giving him the guitar, but that he wanted to split the insurance money, which had to be more than $250. Gibbons huffed and bluffed, saying the guitar was too priceless to have been insured. In any case the happy reunion of Gibbons and his "Hendrix" was newsworthy enough to merit a "Random Note" in *Rolling Stone*.

"For all we know," says a Houston musician, "Jimi Hendrix could have flown into Texas the day before he died and put a guitar in Billy Gibbons' hands." But it didn't happen when anyone else was around.

Nor did Hendrix, as another frequently repeated story has it, go on the *Tonight* show and rave about the young up and coming Texas guitar player, Billy Gibbons. Hendrix did mention the Moving Sidewalks—not Gibbons, specifically—on a New York radio interview shortly after the Texas tour. Betty Paul, Dan Mitchell's girlfriend, who'd moved to New York City to

Coming to a theater near you:
MOTHS ATE MY HAT
GRAFFITI GOT MY GUITAR
BURRITOS SNUCK AROUND
MY WAISTLINE
in "Billy Lets It All Hang Out"

pursue a career as an artist, heard it, and excitedly told people back home.

"In every one of these stories, there's a half truth," says one of the Tanglewood gang. The funny thing, as most of Billy's old friends agree, is that the real stories are often better than the made-up ones.

Billy rarely talks about the time he and the Sidewalks were rehearsing at the Catacombs, a club run by Richard Ames. Robert Duncan and Don Lampton were squiring Clapton around Houston after his Coliseum show during the 1969 Cream Farewell Tour. After Clapton had gotten the western clothes and Mexican food he'd requested, Duncan and Lampton decided to take him by the club. The Sidewalks were charging full-tilt through "Crossroads," which Lampton describes as "one of their better songs at the time. Billy could really play 'Crossroads'." The stage lights were on, so the Sidewalks had no idea that the shadowy figure in the back wasn't just a bartender or a beer delivery boy who frequented the joint during the day.

"When the song was over," Lampton continues, "without me or anyone else prompting him, Clapton just walks right up onstage and shakes Gibbons' hand."

And what did Billy do?

"Well, that's the priceless story. You should have seen the expressions on the faces of the group!"

While the rest of the band verged on collective cardiac arrest, Billy took his famous guest star's praise in stride. He and Clapton spent the rest of the afternoon talking about blues and guitars. Billy had received the Bluesplayer's Seal of Approval.

CHAPTER 3

THE MOVING SIDEWALKS... MOVING

BUT even as the Sidewalks and their buddies spent their afternoons by the pool, jabbering about not only shaking hands with stars like Clapton and Hendrix, but joining them in the firmament, the Pentagon was making its own psychedelic plans for boys like Billy Gibbons. At 19 and 20, the Tanglewood Factory types were prime for Vietnam. Most of them, including Gibbons, maintained some sort of student-deferment status at local colleges.

Gibbons' enrollment in the University of Texas kept him away from the draft board. At UT, he made some pretense of studying art. Gibbons is a very witty, talented cartoonist who probably could have worked in some professional capacity. But once he'd experienced the sheer, intoxicating buzz of playing on a concert stage, and hearing the applause, there was little question about his career moves. It sure wasn't homework.

Tom Moore, the Sidewalks' keyboard player, and Don Summers, the bassist, weren't so lucky, scared, or so full of conscientious objections. Uncle Sam called and they went. But even if Moore and Summers hadn't been drafted, the Sidewalks, despite their local popularity, might have been doomed anyway.

With the exception of "99th Floor," which is powered by sheer exuberance alone, most of the material the Sidewalks recorded on several singles and one local album was pretty mediocre, primitively produced approximations of the trends of the day. But then again, they were only kids, just learning how to play and use the studio. It was enough that they were able to play in tune, in time, and to express a rough idea or two. Their producer, Steve Ames, who lacked the vision and experience of industry hotshots on either coast, couldn't really take them any further.

The backwards guitar, out-of-phase pick-ups, echoey vocals and feedback that leap out of the Sidewalks' songs were the same psychedelights young musicians all over the world were discovering. The joy and wonder of their experimentation still shines through, even if today much of the Sidewalks' material is as awkward and dated as their paisley prints and bellbottom, flower power costumes.

Most of the Sidewalks' stuff—like a tedious, psychedelic version

Is this the face of a discriminating collector of modern art? Billy demonstrates sheer intoxicating buzz on the *El Loco* tour.

of "I Want To Hold Your Hand"—is weighted down by a stiff beat, and even stiffer organ. There's really only one genuine talent, Gibbons, on these early cuts, and he hadn't yet developed the richness or expressiveness of vocal or guitar tone. The Hendrix licks Gibbons was trying to master during the last days of the Sidewalks may sound thin and forced because of Gibbons' (and his producer's) lack of studio sophistication. But more likely, although Hendrix was steeped as was Gibbons, in R&B and blues, Jimi's style was never a comfortable mode for Billy. Gibbons' Tanglewood buddies say Billy's playing really changed and improved when he began listening to Fleetwood Mac's Peter Green. They think Green influenced him more than any other guitarist. That may be partly true, but their similar approach may stem from the fact that both Green and Gibbons are white boys who found in the blues the language of their hearts. It wasn't until Gibbons went back to his own raw, natural, unpsychedelicized roots that he really started to talk.

Dusty and Frank meet the Maharishi.

Despite the Sidewalks' short-comings as recording artists, it's not impossible to understand how their songs might play live: especially when accompanied by strobe lights, explosions, pivoting guitars and assorted antics, or when most of the audience was probably on acid. In those days nearly everything sounded new and promising.

However, Billy, unlike most of his audience and most of the musicians he played with, never went through a serious drug phase. Billy acknowledges that he may have dropped acid a few times, but the only real phase anyone remembers him going through was transcendental meditation. In the early 1970s, when the tour stopped, Billy went off to meet the Maharishi and TM became his first priority. But, for the most part, Billy didn't need drugs or anything else. He was just out there.

His innate strangeness drew him originally to Lanier Greig, the keyboard player for Neil Ford & the Fanatics. After Tom Moore was drafted, Lanier sat in on several gigs. He was Billy's equal as a gifted musician, but, more important, he was a practical joker, too. One night Lanier went down to the Cellar, a strip joint where a Dallas band called the American Blues was accompanying the gyrations of the female talent. Greig said his name was "Billy Gibbons" to the bassplayer Dusty Hill and drummer Frank Beard. He asked if he could sit in and jam. Greig, a stranger to guitar playing, picked up the instrument and proceeded to destroy Gibbons' local reputation.

Billy didn't mind, In fact, he thought he might go down to the Cellar and jam on keyboards with the American Blues, calling himself "Lanier." He just never got around to it. He was busy with other stunts. He and Lanier drove an old pick-up truck around town. They would alternate between driving and taking turns on the drum kit in the bed of the truck. Once they rented white tuxedos and put on whiteface, black noses and huge ears that were cut from old records. The dynamic duo would go over to Herman Park to see what kind of crowd they could draw.

Sometimes he and Greig would drive to Gracie's Chicken Farm, a famous whorehouse. They weren't interested in sampling the merchandise, they were there on a "mission for God." The Chicken Farm appealed to Gibbons—he thought it might make good material for a song. He just hadn't figured out how to write—or sing it—yet. That's why they drove all over the countryside, from one barbecue stand to the next. It wasn't only for the greasy roadside food—although Gibbons was a connoisseur—but to observe the black country people who frequented them. To try and get their accents, their stance, down. There was one particular place in Richmond that Billy really liked. There was one old black guy who sang for bottles of wine. When he went "how, how, how," it was as good as Howlin' Wolf. It was just the voice Billy needed for the song about Gracie's Chicken Farm that legions of ZZ Top fans later came to know and love as "La Grange."

Their mutual delight in such excursions convinced Billy that he and Greig ought to form a new group, along with Dan Mitchell, the only other Sidewalk who managed to stay out of the army.

Power to the people: An early sticker with a ZZ chant.

ZZ ★ TOP ★ FOR PRESIDENT

CHAPTER 4

ZZ's
BEGINNINGS

FROM the start, there were really more than three of them. Dan Mitchell originally suggested they ask Bill Ham to manage the band. Gibbons' version of their first meeting takes place at the Doors' show in Houston, where the Sidewalks and their spinning guitars got the standing ovation. Gibbons says Ham walked up to him, offered him a cigar and said he'd make him a star. Dan Mitchell said they first encountered Ham earlier, when the Sidewalks backed up a Bluesbreaker-less John Mayall.

Bill Ham once had ambitions as a singer. He recorded at least one single for Dot Records. Few remember the song name, only that it was awful. Ham was a crooner in the Pat Boone mold. Boone was not only an inspiration, but also a friend of Ham's from Dallas. Ham later worked for Dot Records as a promotion man. When he met this Sidewalks, he was promoting for Daily Record Distributors in Houston.

Those who knew Ham in his promo days don't remember him breaking any specific acts in Texas. They do recall his erratic behavior. He would frequently disappear for days, remaining secre-tive about his whereabouts, work odd hours, and not return phone calls. He would return from one of his disappearances, phone a record store and scream that a record was not displayed prominently enough or to his satisfaction. Once, he rushed out of the office in a fury, stacked a pile of albums on top of his convertible and drove down the street, records flying behind him. It was not exactly the method of distribution his bosses had in mind. But the Sidewalks were immediately impressed with his record biz rap, promo-man acumen, and enthusiasm.

Ham was looking for a band with whom he could play the role of another of his models, Colonel Tom Parker, Elvis Presley's manager. He talked incessantly about the Colonel. He may have gleaned some inside info about the Colonel's operation from Gabe Tucker, who lived in Houston and had worked for Parker for many years. Tucker's wife, Sunshine, was also receptionist for the Daily brothers. In any case, Ham had definite ideas about what the band would have to do to make it, and how he would sell it. And even in the beginning, before the band was generating enough revenue to dine

ZZ Meltdown, celebrating the release of *Deguello*.

at a roadside barbecue, Ham was talking about the ways he planned to invest his coming fortune in oil leases and Stop & Go markets.

He decided they needed an idea that was different: not necessarily a different sound but a different image. For a while, they thought they might say they came from England, but that wouldn't work. They might be more believable as three old blues guys. Ham was sure about one thing: the music shouldn't be too progressive. He wanted to keep it simple. Ham knew what he liked, according to Lanier Greig, and he knew what would sell. The bigger the secret, the better. Before they recorded a single note, Ham planned to make the world wait indefinitely for subsequent album releases. He knew how badly people would try to get hold of him when he disappeared. The phone messages would be piled in little mountains. By creating a mystery, an inaccessibility, the public would be desperate to get their hands on the band's next release. Make them beg!

But what would they beg *for*?

Dan Mitchell remembers the concept that was settled on: "We were supposed to look like three old men, three bums, and get up and knock everybody's lights out. We weren't supposed to shave for a day. In the original publicity photos, we looked really scruffy."

Lanier Greig adds, "We decided the album would be called *Back Down in the Alley*, and we'd be laying down in the alley with trash cans and dressed in Salvation Army clothes."

They needed a blues name to go with the blues image. No wonder current members of ZZ Top don't know what the band's name means.

When questioned about its origins today: they didn't make it up. According to Lanier, the trio's name was born in the hippie pad Dan Mitchell and Billy shared at one point. They took Z. Z. Hill's name from a poster, one of many photos of their blues heroes on the apartment's walls. The "Top" came from a package of rolling papers.

Gibbons, Greig and Mitchell went down to the Paris County Courthouse to register the name. They never did copyright the material they worked on for several months, though much of which appeared on ZZ Top's *First Album*.

When they left for Robin Hood, Brian's recording studio in Tyler, Tex., to record their first single, "Salt Lick" b/w "Miller's Farm" (paid for by Bill Ham's employers, the Dailys), Ham convinced Greig it would be better if they left his name off the credits. Ham started (and ended) his own label, "Scat Records" for the "Salt Lick/Miller's Farm" single. Greig was signed to Acuff-Rose publishing, and they'd owe them a percentage. According to Greig, Ham promised they'd work something out. Billy even gave Lanier a piece of paper, saying he bequeathed him half of the royalties from "Salt Lick" and "Miller's Farm." The lawyer Greig once took it to told him it wasn't a legal document. Which was too bad, because not much later, Greig got a call from songwriter Jeff Barry in New York, who was casting a pilot for a Monkees-style television show called *The Cowboys*. Greig, who is a talented Robin Williams-style comedian as well as a gifted keyboard player, couldn't pass up the opportunity. So he went to New York for a few days, thinking the band would understand. Instead, they felt he was a traitor to the ZZ cause. When he got back to Texas, he got a call from Billy. Rather than tell Greig he was being kicked out of the band, Billy made up some story that he was going to quit. Greig got the picture and left. As it turns out, Greig was written out of *The Cowboys* script. The show never made it past the pilot stage.

Greig has never made a stink about the songwriting credits, royalties or his ownership of the name. He gave up the name without a fight because Bill Ham told him he wouldn't want to hold them back. After all, Lanier always thought Ham and Gibbons would do the right thing when the time came. He and his buddy Billy had a deal from the start. When they used to drive out to the country and eat barbecue, they talked about the future and what would happen if one made it before the other. Ironically, Greig, who had done some session work on both coasts but never really made it financially, almost ended up sleeping in the alley and living the blues bum life that he and Billy Gibbons had studied on field trips.

Lanier didn't even get the six-pack of beer Bill Ham promised the boys as payment for their first single. On the return from the session at Brian's Robin Hood studio in Tyler (where ZZ has recorded throughout the years) they got arrested. It was not only a dry county, but two of them were minors as well.

Dan Mitchell lasted a little longer. He and Billy recruited Billy Ethridge, the Dallas-based Chessmen's former bassplayer, and kept playing as ZZ Top. Mitchell claims to have contributed to material on the first, if not subsequent, albums. Like Lanier, he was never compensated for writing, playing on "Salt Lick" or for owning the name, either. It's particularly painful, not only because he and Billy were such long-time friends, but because he feels the single helped get the next ZZ Top their contract with London Records. But, like Greig, he always felt that Ham and Gibbons would do the "right thing," and if nothing else, help with a future musical endeavor. Both musicians had later bands that they feel might have gotten the major label deals they came close to signing, if someone had put in a favorable word. No one did. They're still waiting. Billy's not talking.

Dan Mitchell knew the end was near when he walked into rehearsal one day and found the American Blues' Frank Beard, an old Dallas friend of Billy Ethridge's playing his drumset. They were just jamming, supposedly, but soon Mitchell was replaced for good. No one remembers what happened to Billy Ethridge.

Says one of the Tanglewood musicians, "Maybe like so many kids in a strange town without even a bank or a credit card, he was just broke and homesick and went home. We were boys then, not men."

The first meeting of the eventual supergroup was not particularly promising. Frank Beard had been trying to get Billy together with Dusty Hill for the longest time. Beard played—and dyed his hair blue—with Dusty and his brother Rocky Hill in the American Blues. Dusty remembers two singles from those heady days: "Captain Fire" and "Chocolate Ego". American

continued on and off for about three years.

However, getting Dusty, Frank and Billy together is no simple maneuver. Something always came up. Or Billy wouldn't show up. He was almost as elusive as Ham. The night he finally did appear, Frank and Dusty had given up on the idea of jamming and drank a prodigious amount of cheap wine. When Billy finally arrived about four hours later, Dusty had just enough energy to lift his head off the couch mid-slumber and whisper a groggy "hi." Billy looked at Frank and then Dusty and back again and wondered—so that's the guy?

CHAPTER 5

DUSTY

DUSTY's origins were as humble as Billy's were affluent. They have so little in common, other than facial hair, one little white lie Dusty tells (he says his real name's Dusty; it's Joe) and an overwhelming compulsion to wiggle their knees and duckwalk in front of thousands of people every night. It's almost amazing they've been performing together for nearly 15 years.

The son of a truckdriver, Dusty (whose real name is Joe) was raised in Dallas by his mother, who worked as a waitress and his stepfather, who worked at a Ford plant. Like Billy, he has a half sister who's considerably older. She's now a schoolteacher. He has a half brother, an antiques dealer. A sister died at 36 from alcoholism. "She hit it," Dusty says, "pretty good." His older brother Rocky, with whom Dusty played for most of his pre-ZZ career, is a blues-oriented guitar player who's never been as lucky, or as willing, to take direction as Dusty has. Dusty's always felt badly that Rocky hasn't achieved his professional success. He thinks his brother is the more talented. People who know them both do not disagree.

Unlike Gibbons' parents, Mrs. Dusty (as she's known around the ZZ camp) never frowned upon rock'n'roll. She loved it.

"She bought the records," explains Dusty. "Rock'n'roll, blues, big band, Lightnin' Hopkins, Elvis, Little Richard. There was always a lot of music around the house."

Mrs. Dusty had been a singer herself, although she'd never recorded and had abandoned any big-time showbiz aspirations well before Dusty was born. But she always encouraged him.

When he was 8 Dusty traded the guitar he'd gotten for Christmas for Rocky's present, a bicycle.

"He learned how to play the guitar," Dusty remembers, "I almost broke my neck on the bicycle." When Dusty gave up the bike for a mike, he and Rocky started doing Elvis and Little Richard impersonations in the places his mother worked. As he describes them, they were "cafes in the afternoon and beer joints at night." Dusty and Rocky's first appearances were in the afternoons. Eventually they worked their way up to beer-joint time.

When his brother wanted to start a band, Dusty began playing bass.

"Take that, Pete Townsend!"
Dusty in *Eliminator* action stance.

Dusty finally had to replace his beloved tin foil-backed Telecaster bass with a custom-made model.

Six" one of his more recent. His singing (or shouting) has changed little since he jumped on the pooltable as a little boy and did Little Richard.

Dusty and Rocky's first band was called the Starliners. The next was the Deadbeats, who were responsible for what he considers one of the great mistakes of his life. He dropped out of school.

"In ninth grade, I flunked English, cause I just didn't care," he remembers. "So they were gonna send me to summer school. About two weeks in, I went 'screw this,' cause I was playin' gigs. Just before the school year started, they gave me this booklet, and I took a test. So I start the school year, and I got the chance to play a few days in Tennessee. Wound up stayin' about two weeks. Then I go to school and they want to know where I've been. My mother will not lie. She said, I took you up there, it was on the up and up. So she wrote it all out and I took the paper and they wouldn't accept it. And they said I had to do all these detentions, which I always had a shitload of anyhow. So I said, "What? I'm gonna get punished for telling the truth? And I went, well, screw you. And that was a lousy attitude to have, but it pissed me off. Had my mother wrote that I'd broken my leg they would have said okay."

Dusty regrets his lack of formal education, and rarely mentions it because, "I don't want anyone to get the idea it's the way to go. Some guy out there in the tenth grade goes oh, 'Dusty's makin all this dough'—cause it's real unusual. It's always been a problem for me. I didn't have enough education to get along."

They already had a guitarist and a drummer, so it was his only option. If Dusty's bassplaying is distinctive, it is because he was never a failed guitarist who approached the bass as a lead instrument. To this day, Dusty has remained essentially a singer who plays bass because it's part of the job. Listen to "Tush," perhaps his most famous vocal performance, or "I Got the

FRANK BEARD

FRANK also dropped out of high school at 15, but not because he didn't bring the correct note to the principal's office. He had to get married, go to work and support his 18-year-old wife and baby daughter.

"It was pretty much a shotgun type of wedding," he remembers. "Her family hated me. I hated them. I hated her. She hated me. My parents hated her and her parents hated my parents. Everybody hated everybody."

Beard's father, officer manager and bookkeeper for a Ford dealership, and mother, who worked at Sears for 25 years, were devastated. In one summer their only son and baby—Frank has an older sister now a claims adjuster for State Farm Insurance—had been transformed into a creature they hardly recognized.

Frank had been playing drums for a couple of years, since he begged his father, who was recovering from an appendix operation, to get out of bed and buy him a drumset at Leonard's department store in Fort Worth. He had a teenage band called "The Hustlers." But the main preoccupaton of his early teens had been football. He was small, but "ultra-fast," like a fly he says.

Frank's favorite drum solo wasn't played on drums. It was the sound of raindrops falling outside his window.

"I was a heavyweight jock, so I got to go out with older women," he explains. "I didn't take any drugs. I didn't smoke, I didn't drink, I didn't do anything. But by the end of the next summer, I was married, out of the house, quit school and working in a strip joint and taking God knows what."

He worked at the International Superstore as assistant manager of the sporting goods department, selling rods and reels and guns during the day. At night, he was playing in the Fort Worth Cellar, which, like the Houston etablishment of the same name, featured female entertainment.

There, Beard "got into the position to do some wild things when I was in the mood to do wild things."

Some of those wild things included dropping acid and dyeing his hair blue with Dusty and Rocky Hill. His young wife and his parents no longer understood him.

"She and I were together when I was one person," says Frank. "And I completely did a flip-over and was not that person anymore. I didn't care about the things I used to care about. I was a stranger to her. And she was not hip. You gotta remember, this is 1966, it's hitting hot and heavy around Texas. The music and drugs and the lifestyle is really setting in. She couldn't make that change."

Beard tried to get a divorce, but his wife was pregnant again.

Frank explains, "In Texas you can't get divorced when you're pregnant." Frank eventually did get a divorce. After years of being subpoenaed to meet his child support every time ZZ Top played, he relinquished his rights to see his children in return for a cash settlement. He's since been reunited with his teenage daughters Denise and Diana. He eventually got a high school equivalency certificate and has since enrolled in a few courses at El Centro Junior College.

CHAPTER 7

DUSTY, FRANK & BILLY

"**I PICKED** up on the fact that Billy was a little strange from the beginning," said Frank Beard.

"When I first met Billy, he had a beard. A little short chinstrap type of beard. I'd never seen a guitar player with a beard before. In 1969, musicians did not have beards. You can't name me one with a beard back in 1969. Not even Gregg Allman. He had the little jazz dot."

But even stranger were his roadies, people who actually carried and took care of his equipment. Frank had never heard of roadies then, and wouldn't have considered hiring one if he had.

"No Dallas bands had roadies," he says. "We carted all our own shit." Frank and his Dallas friends would have rather kept the $10 or $20 they would have had to pay a roadie for themselves. They didn't see themselves as pampered rock stars.

"Dallas musicians were different from Houston musicians. Dallas musicians were tougher, earthier. We were all like Freddie King. We played good blues and would whip your ass. We were tough guys. The Dallas group was more into the music, whereas the Houston group might have been more into the show."

Billy was used to having people do things for him. He came from a more affluent background than either Dusty or Frank, a distinction both Frank and Dusty still note. Billy was also artier. His educational background, and his self identity was that of an artist—a perception neither Dusty or Frank shared.

The differences were even more marked in the early days of ZZ Top, when Frank and Dusty were sharing a garage apartment and says Frank, starving. Billy's parents helped him out. Frank remembers the first winter in Houston as the low point.

"It was a cold winter here in Houston, and we didn't have a telephone, we didn't have a TV. We didn't have shit for shinola. And we were bored. We hadn't seen anybody for four or five days. Couldn't get out of the house. So we scraped up all the bottles in the house, and all the change. All the money we had in the world and we came up with $1.69 or something. We hadn't eaten in two or three days. There was no food, no nothing. We didn't know anybody down here, we didn't have any friends. We walked to the U Tote Em in the dead of cold and bought a gallon of red wine and a roll of toilet paper with our $1.69. We were walking home and Dusty dropped the sack and broke the gallon of wine and soaked the whole roll of toilet paper. I could've killed him. If it wouldn't have been too degrading, I probably would've sucked the toilet paper to get the wine." It took some time before their situation improved radically.

In 1969, after playing constantly all over Texas, ZZ Top recorded their first album. The cost of recording, approximately $12,000, was paid by Bill Ham's employers, Don and H. W. Daily, Jr. To the consternation of his employers, Ham was devoting more and more time to the band. But he kept his job until well after ZZ Top's second album. Frank said, "He believed in the band, but not enough to quit his job." The second album, *Rio Grande Mud*, and a part of the third were also financed by the Dailys.

Ham's connection with Daily Distributors convinced London to sign the band. The Dailys not only paid for the studio time, they assured London they could sell enough records in Texas so that there would be no risk on the label's part. There wasn't a risk, aside from the cost of the album's mastering, pressing and cover art. Ham thought he could get $100,000 from the record company for signing the band. He ended up, according to H. W. Daily, with about $1,000, which infuriated him. The Dailys were never able to reach any agreement on a contract with Ham. Because they put up the cash, they wanted 51% of the profits. Ham wanted it 50-50. After three albums, the Dailys had received nothing.

A lengthy lawsuit followed. The matter was finally settled out of court in 1975 for approximately $100,000, a negligible sum considering their legal costs and the million dollar revenues the band has since earned. The Dailys simply wanted to close the whole tedious and distasteful process. Based on ZZ Top's track record at the time of the settlement, it looked like the band was going nowhere.

"Que pasa, gringos?" The trio in their pre-*American Gigolo* days, long before Frank discovered Giorgio Armani or started selling Fila jogging suits.

ZZ in the early seventies. Note the visit to LaGrange, Texas, far right.

CHAPTER 8

THE RECORDS

"**T**HIS *Texas boogie band enjoyed a vogue during 1975 and 1976, when its concerts broke attendance records set by the Beatles, among others. But on record, ZZ Top was never more than a poor man's Lynyrd Skynrd—some rural feeling but mostly just numbing guitar drive. Rock'n'roll can be mindless fun, but it never deserved to be this empty headed.*"—Dave Marsh, summing up ZZ Top's career, in the *Rolling Stone Record Guide*.

Going back to ZZ Top's early London albums, it's not hard to understand why their records didn't appeal either to critics or to a mass audience at the time. They weren't very good.

On ZZ Top's *First Album*, the band sounds as if they're wrestling with their new identity as "blues guys." The material was not particularly distinguished or focused white blues, the production quality was even worse. Bill Ham, who received credit for co-writing four of the album's ten tracks, was no more technically accomplished or creatively inspired than Steve Ames.

Prefacing the album was this explanatory liner note: "In this day of homogenized rock, synthesized music, retakes, overdubbing, multi, multi-tracking, an honest recording by accomplished musicians is a rewarding pleasure. ZZ Top's *First Album* is just such a recording. This is the way blues rock is meant to be played: openly, honestly and spontaneously. It takes an experienced sensitive group such as ZZ Top to capture the *abstract blues* from within and combine it with the ability to feel and play good hard rock without losing their communication."

It was captioned, oddly, "abstract blues," as if it were part of some greater treatise and signed, mysteriously, "From Friends."

The rationale was to present the band as the "real thing," a bunch of backwoods buddies brought straight from a hot jam out in the shed. Of course, if Ham had announced that this group was the next Beatles, the next Stones, the next Elvis, the result would have been an immediate turn-off. The tactic was under, rather than over-hype. The liner note had another effect. It was almost an excuse for the ragged content and poor technical quality of the tracks.

Of course, the band had been together for only a few months before recording the first album, so

Who would guess Billy is insecure about his slide playing?

perhaps it's unrealistic to expect cohesive material. It sounds as if their jams had been structured into strings or riffs. It was 1970, a time when preproduction meant rehearsing—not refining—songs before recording them. At best, early ZZ Top sounds like a Texas Cream. Dusty's elementary bass lines sound as if they were played in a swamp. Dusty was not as nimble as Jack Bruce, and Frank's playing isn't particularly sharp or volatile, either. It may have had to do with the way his drums were muffled and recorded.

Instrumentally, the burden was on Gibbons, and especially since there were few, if any, guitar overdubs. But Gibbons, on the *First Album*, sounds intent on proving he can play every lick in the Eric Clapton songbook, even the inappropriate ones. On "Old Man," his incessant lead fights against the vocal melody. But that may be what Gibbons was encouraged to do. It's the producer's job to know when less is more. And in this case, the producer didn't have the slightest idea.

The bluesmen Gibbons obsequiously mimics in his vocals—Bobby (Blue) Bland, B. B. King—could pull off an average number like "Just Got Back from Baby's" or "Backdoor Love Affair" by investing it with a genuine knowledge. Billy sounds like a smart-ass college boy doing Amos'n'Andy, not like a devoted student of the genre.

Rio Grande Mud, the band's second effort, is notable as the only ZZ Top album that has ever acknowledged a musician other than Gibbons, Beard and Hill. Pete Tickle, Billy Gibbons' roadie in Moving Sidewalks' days and ZZ Top's road manager for 14 years,

played acoustic guitar on *Mushmouth Blues*.

One of the rarely told ZZ stories, is how Pete Tickle got his name. Pete Tickle's real name is Bill. Through the years, those who dealt with Tickle assumed the ZZ family called him Pete to avoid confusion with Bill Ham or Billy Gibbons. Pete Tickle actually got his name back in the days of the Moving Sidewalks, when the Tanglewood gang gathered in front of the stage at the Ames' club, "like little groupies," to watch one of their idols, Jeff Beck. Rod Stewart was the singer. A man named Pete was the roadie. Beck, who's known as a temperamental character, kept shouting at his roadie, "Pete! Go over and get this! Come here and do this!" The performance made a great impression on Billy Gibbons. The next time the Sidewalks played, he began calling Bill Tickle "Pete" and the name stuck.

Rio Grande Mud is notable for another credit, on "Francine," perhaps the album's most commercial song and a single at the time of its release in 1973. It was co-written by Kenny Cordray and Steve Perron. Actually, in a move owing more to Gibbons' eccentricity than his generosity toward his Mexican amigos, "Francine" was sung in English on one side of the 45, Spanish on the other. To this day, Billy speaks Spanish *con mucho gusto*. The results are usually as amusing as the bilingual version of "Francine".

But he doesn't like to credit his collaborators. It was the only time that Gibbons' co-workers outside the band were given part of their due. Steve Perron died shortly after the band recorded "Francine," and his widow, Linda, says

Billy gets loose in 1983.

she's never received royalties.

In fact, Billy's actual contribution to the writing of "Francine" is debatable. The original song was written by Perron and Cordray, who were playing with the Children at the time. Gibbons sat in with Children when Kenny Cordray, their guitar player, was injured in an accident. He fell in love with "Francine." Gibbons rearranged the song, apparently when he played it with Children. Whether the structural changes were significant enough to claim authorship is questionable. "Francine" remained essentially Steve Perron's song.

Perron is even mentioned in the song, in the line "If I catch her with Stevie P." When Children played "Francine," Perron sang "If I catch her with Billy G." Dusty says the lyric has provided ZZ several laughs over the years. He remembers seeing a Mexican bar band playing a cover version of "Francine," and feeling that ZZ Top must be making it if they were already being covered. The band was doing the English version, though. When Dusty went up to congratulate them on their peformance, they responded with blank looks. He realized that they'd learned the song phonetically. They couldn't speak English. They had almost everything but the "Stevie P." reference right. The translators of lyrics for the Japanese release of *Rio Grande Mud* also had a hard time figuring out what "Stevie P." was. They filled in the blank with an image of their own device.

The real Stevie P. was a genius (with an IQ of 180), who died from a fatal combination of a few drinks with friends and the painkillers he was taking for a hernia condition.

Fred and Ginger never duck-walked like this duo.

His widow, Linda, says that reports he choked on a sandwich or fishstick or killed himself because he was depressed over his lack of recognition as a songwriter were untrue.

Perron was independently wealthy. Children were in the process of recording for Ode, and Steve was optimistic and full of plans when he died. Full of songs, too. Another song he had written was "Master of Sparks." Linda Perron isn't sure if it's the same "Master of Sparks" Billy Gibbons claims to have written and appears on ZZ Top's third album, *Tres Hombres*.

She does know that Billy's song was inspired by something one of Steve Perron's friends supposedly did and he told Billy about. Billy and Perron may have seen the friend perform the pointless stunt that Gibbons' "Master of Sparks" describes. Linda says she always thought "Steve was pulling my leg. He was like Billy that way."

The protagonist of Billy's song goes out to a deserted country road where he is strapped into a custom-made steel cage and thrown off the back of a pick-up truck for thrills.

Whether or not Steve Perron and Billy Gibbons ever witnessed any-

one being thrown off a truck in a "Sparks"-like incident is debatable. But everyone who knew Billy is pretty sure that he was never dragged, sparks flying from the metal on asphalt. It may have been one of the more outlandish examples of his liking a friend's story so much he decided to borrow it.

"Just Got Paid," another of the stronger selections on *Rio Grande Mud* met an unusual fate. Every time ZZ played it, fans would customarily throw change at the stage. "Just Got Paid" eventually became too dangerous to perform. Money thrown in a small hall can cause a few black-and-blues. But when it's tossed off a balcony, a quarter can gather enough velocity to cause serious damage. So "Just Got Paid" had to be retired from the live show. "We had to make the decision," says Billy, "whether the fifty dollars or so extra we'd pick up in spare change a night was worth it." When Gibbons wrote the song, ZZ probably needed every speeding penny thrown their way. With the next album, the situation began to improve somewhat.

On *Tres Hombres*, Billy's stories may have started to head toward the twilight zone. However, he was beginning to find his sound and his voice on record. Perhaps it was a change of engineers and studios. They went to Ardent in Memphis and used engineer Terry Manning for the first time. Manning had engineered Led Zeppelin, and brought a directness, an immediacy, to their sound. The difference between *Tres Hombres* sound quality and anything ZZ Top had done previously was almost astounding.

The songwriting was also getting sharper, tighter and more professional.

La Grange retained the blues essence, but the feel is more contemporary. There's a rumor that Canned Heat was upset with ZZ Top for copping their "Fried Hockey Boogie," but the riff is really Slim Harpo's via the Stones. Just put it up next to "Shake Your Hips" on *Exile on Main Street*.

The band was finally able to get their concept and their humor across, too. The Tex-Mex combination plate on the inside cover was the visual equivalent of the songs' spirit: greasy, salty and spicy. "Shiek" is notable for Billy's rare use of a wah-wah pedal. On "Beerdrinkers and Hellraisers" it sounds as if the band had pinpointed their audience. It represents the first break with the awkward blues that had dominated their previous efforts. They were learning how to write material that would appeal to a group beyond the habitues of a easily impressed bar and small-town concert scene. It was their first bona fide anthem.

Tres Hombres was their first record to make serious money. Frank remembers getting a royalty check for $72,000, more money than he'd ever dreamed of. He had once thought he'd be rolling in clover if he could scrape together $50,000. That'd be enough to live on for awhile. Dusty had similar visions. After all, it'd take a lot of return bottles to come up with that kind of dough. With $50,000 in the bank they could be sure that when they next had an accident on the way back from U Tote Em, they'd be able to go back for more toilet paper.

Bill Ham always had grander schemes. He didn't just want purchasing power at the U Tote Em, he wanted to own the whole shopping

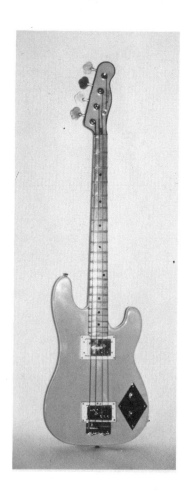

Bell bottom blues? Billy models the upwardly-mobile cowboy look of the *Worldwide Texas Tour.*

mall. The only way to achieve that, especially without a real smash-hit record, was to tour. ZZ's schedule was becoming grueling, some 300 nights a year. When they had to, they slept in the van, or on floors. They opened for bands who were on their last legs—like Mott the Hoople and Alice Cooper, who were making one final attempt to clean up on the road before packing it in. Mott didn't care what the opening act did. So ZZ Top went out and blew them away. They knew the kids wouldn't forget.

But, unless ZZ figured how to channel the energy of their increasingly popular live show to vinyl, success would remain remote. The answer was *Fandango!*.

One side was recorded live at the Warehouse in New Orleans; the other sounds as if it was recorded almost live in the studio. Ham credited himself for the "concept" and stuck on a little note, an echo of the first album's introductory message: This music is brought to you honestly, without the assistance of studio gimmicks.

At the time, it was unusual to record a live album that wasn't a greatest hits package. It reflected Ham's—and the band's—increasing frustration at being stuck in the regional minor leagues, and shut out of the national airwaves. The inner sleeve featured a photo of ZZ's biggest gig—an 80,000-seat outdoor show in Austin. It was an effort to show the rest of the world who they were, and how big they were. ZZ also started emphasizing their regionalism, calling themselves "that little old band from Texas" and wearing flamboyant, brocaded Nudie suits.

Lanier says he had first suggested suits in 1969, when the band started, but the idea was shelved in favor of the "bum" look. Cost may have also been a factor. ZZ's Nudie suits cost upward of $1,300 each. In the early days, the band wasn't making that much a night. The Nudie era may have represented the beginning of Frank Beard's sartorial break with Dusty and Billy. It's almost physically impossible to play drums wearing the heavily brocaded costume. Insiders suggest the real reason Billy put on a cowboy outfit was that he was becoming self-conscious about losing his hair and wanted to wear a hat. In the early 1970s a potential rock star, whether from Texas or Timbucktu, had to have a glorious, full head of hair. But the Nudie suits finally gave the band a definite visual hook, a recognizable image distinguishing them from other jeans-and-flannel Southern bands they were compared with. More important, they were beginning to develop a distinct sound, one that played off and exploited their regionalism. "I Heard It On the X" captured the wonder of learning rock licks from an outlaw station across the Mexican border. It doesn't matter if the story is true or not, it sounds as if it is. Dusty and Billy traded vocals the way they do onstage. It sounds like they're elbowing each other at the mike while exchanging wicked glances. Billy does most of the vocals on the record, and Dusty takes half of them onstage, but here Dusty got his part on vinyl. No explanatory liner notes necessary, you can hear the spontaneity and authenticity.

"Balinese" is supposedly about a ballroom where Billy's father played. "Mexican Blackbird" is probably another of his fabrications (about a black Mexican

Signs of the times: Frank's nursing a beer and the costume trunks are jam-packed with Nudie suits.

prostitute), but it's remarkable for Gibbons' twangy cowboy vocal. It's a brilliant bit of comic mimicry. With his great ear, gift for accents and comedic flair, it sometimes seems like Gibbons missed his true calling as a character actor. But the way video and rock are transforming the movie industry, perhaps he'll find it yet. Hollywood hasn't had a singing cowboy in a long

time, and they've never had one so off-the-wall or so demented as this dude.

Back in the *Fandango!* days, Gibbons was busy inciting his audience to "Get high, everybody, get high!" "Thunderbird" was another sop to the hell-raisers and to cheap-wine drinkers. Given their reliance on party hymns for the boogie republic, it's little wonder critics like

Dave Marsh concluded that their numbing guitar was also numb-skull-ish. But *Fandango!*'s reverent covers of "Jailhouse Rock" and Willie Dixon's "Mellow Down Easy" connected the band firmly to its roots.

But the song that tied ZZ's and its audience's aspirations together in two minutes and fourteen seconds of steamy, sweaty and sloppy inspiration was "Tush."

Like "Louie, Louie," an earlier bump, grind and grunge classic, "Tush" is ridiculous, simple and sublime. Anyone can sing it, anyone can play it, and everyone can relate to it. ZZ barrels along, combining straight-ahead "Francine"-style rhythm with Billy's best slide and Dusty's best Little Richard. He's going downtown looking for

what Little Richard wanted when he wailed that "Miss Molly sure likes to ball." But Dusty adds an extra dimension of terror when he screams, "Take me back, not alone." It's the same feeling known by everyone who goes hunting in bars where "Tush" became the standard of cover bands and jukeboxes.

It was perfect. Years later it provided the right touch of atmosphere-when it accompanied the barfight scene in the film *An Officer and a Gentleman*. John Belushi (for whom it seemed tailor-made) sang it in *Old Boyfriends*. Belushi's performance, incidentally, impressed Dusty, who says not everyone can sing it in the original, high key.

"Tush" also pointed up the differences between the Texans and Eastern cities. No Eastern critic (or linguist) could understand a band that rhymed "tush" with "much," but they had to admire their ingenuity.

Dusty, who's credited with coming up with the lyrics during a soundcheck in Alabama (it may be the only ZZ song that everyone gives him credit for) explained the song's origins.

"In Dallas, 'tush' meant plush. Something fine. Like we have another expression, 'that's a cherry short,' which would mean that's a fine car. But it could mean what you think of back East—'tushy,' It could have a double meaning, like that's a 'tush tush.' "

Fandango! emphasized the ever widening gap between critical and public opinion of ZZ. Even as the band was beginning to shatter box office records around the country, they were routinely written off by the press. On June 9, 1974, they broke Elvis' record at the Nashville State Fairgrounds. On September 23, 1974, they broke the Rolling Stones' record at the Long Beach Arena in California. On July 3, 1975, they outdrew Leon Russell in his Tulsa hometown, at the State Fairgrounds. On July 26, 1975, they broke Led Zeppelin's record at New Orleans' City Park Stadium.

Bobby Abrams' piece in the September 16, 1975 issue of *Phonograph Record* summed up ZZ's situation well.

It began with a quote from an anonymous "leading rock critic": "They're grating, repetitious, hackneyed, and boring. They play material that's been done to death a thousand times. I certainly don't listen to them—does anybody?"

Abrams continued, "It's obvious that the above is representative of most of the media feelings about what is fast becoming the hottest concert act in America." Abrams went on to describe the trio's blistering two hour set, which brought the crowd near the "rioting point."

In the same article, Billy Gibbons confided, "We're still learning about a studio, and we're anxious to learn. But it's a time consuming process, so we're still concentrating on what we know best" (i.e., the live show).

But despite the recording lessons they were learning with "Tush" and *Fandango!*, and their A-student status in the arenas, *Tejas*, ZZ's next studio album, in 1976, reflected the band's confusion.

Ham credited himself again for the "concept" as well as the production. The sound (the album was engineered by Terry Manning) was getting progressively cleaner, but

there are only two really solid songs. With "It's Only Love," they sound as if they're trying, almost a bit too hard, to come up with a commercial Southern rock song, something guaranteed to get radio play. It was a little too pretty, poppy and sterile perhaps for the boogie crowd clamoring for another "Tush." Those fans had to be satisfied with "Arrested for Driving While Blind," a hit single whose subject matter was in the ever popular beer drinking, hell-raising vein.

Gibbons was so eager to please that segment of his audience (actually, it wasn't a segment, it *was* their audience) that he appropriated the title and basis of the song from his friend Kurt Linhof, who says he came up with it. Linhof also says that Gibbons eventually did pay him $500 for his share of the song. The sum probably accounts for the most minute fraction of the royalties Gibbons himself has received for "Arrested." The rest of *Tejas* is not particularly memorable, and, in the case of the klutzy "Snappy Kakkie" and "Enjoy and Get It On," hardly enjoyable.

CHAPTER 9

THE TEXAS TOUR

DESPITE the uneven quality of the *Tejas* album, it launched one of the most talked-about spectacles in rock 'n' roll. Frank Beard explained how the Worldwide Texas Tour evolved.

"We were all sittin' around trying to big-girl each other," he said. "Big girl" is Texan for one-upmanship, and the 1976 Worldwide Texas Tour certainly one-upped them all. The Stones, Bowie—the acts with the resources to put on a big show—never came up with anything even nearly like it. The trailers were part of the act—five semis that were painted to provide a rolling panorama of Texas as they moved down the highway. The Texas-shaped stage was 3,000 square feet and weighed 35 tons. All in all, there were about 75 tons of equipment. At the time it was the most equipment ever taken on the road. A longhorn steer and a buffalo rose on either side of the stage on hydraulic lifts. The lifts were necessary, because, as Beard asked, "Have you ever seen a buffalo leave the stage when it doesn't want to?"

The show began when a pinpoint spotlight hit a lone, howling wolf. The wolf didn't make it through the entire 18-month crusade, however. The circus trainer hired to coach and handle the animals played ZZ Top records to the menagerie for weeks to prepare them for their rock debuts. The wolf became such a trouper that all it wanted to do was sit onstage and shake hands. The wolf was eventually replaced by a tape recording.

There were cacti and corrals and five tethered buzzards. The band didn't find performing with animals a problem, except that, says Beard, "You had to move pretty fast or those buzzards thought you were dinner!"

The rattlesnakes were one unfortunate casualty. Photographers standing in the orchestra pit below the rattlesnakes' plexiglass dome remember how the snakes would hiss when the band was cooking. Overly sensitive to vibrations, the snakes must have thought it was the end of the world each time the bank kicked into their off-the-Richter-scale version of "Tush." A little havelina pig never appeared onstage, but was just a pet, a band mascot. It would hang out in the dressing room with the band as they tuned up or did interviews.

Beard says their one mistake was that the show was too big and

Hill, Gibbons and plastic-domed pets: Snake, rattle and roll.

difficult to mount. It could only be worked once every three nights (it took that long for the trucks to travel between cities and for the crew to set it up). As a result, Beard says, the tour ended up in the red.

Chet Flippo covered the Texas Tour for *Rolling Stone*. His account in the Aug. 26, 1976 issue, includes a rare appearance by Bill Ham and gives a pretty good, on-the-scene picture of the manager and the band.

Flippo caught up with the band in New Orleans' Sugar Bowl where ZZ Top's appearance was prefaced by a five minute mini-riot sparked by a tide of police making drug busts in the Sugar Bowl crowd.

Before the show, Flippo managed to catch up with Bill Ham. Ham reminded the *Rolling Stone* reporter of Presidential candidate Jimmy Carter. Describing Ham as a "bearish wunderkind from Houston," Flippo quotes him:

" 'We played a lot of the out-of-the-way places, playing for the people at people's prices. It's harder that way and takes much longer, but once the band has established itself as a people's band, the people won't leave you.' As Ham gets expansive in his recounting of the long road they've taken together and the many obstacles they've surmounted, he gets to sound very much like Jimmy Carter in his acceptance speech. Indeed, take Carter's acceptance speech and substitute the word 'music' for 'politics' or 'government,' and the word 'concert' for 'primary,' and you get a fair idea of the intensity of Ham's long crusade:

" *[This] will be the year when we give the music of this country back to the people of this country. This year we have had 30 concerts, more than ever before, making it possible to take our campaign directly to the people of America. This has been a long and personal campaign—a humbling experience, reminding us that ultimate music influence rests not with the power brokers but with the people."*

Flippo went on to say that Ham himself had become quite a power broker, "albeit a cautious one." Ham agreed that the mammoth tour had, in fact, been planned as carefully as Carter's 1976 run for the White House. He planned for a year, carefully selecting the right arenas, sending key advance men ahead, "stroking the radio stations," and traveling with his 75-ton entourage. Ham traveled, Flippo said, with "the constant fear and knowledge that his career is on the line if he has planned wrong or if he fucks up. An elaborate staging that purports to take Texas to the world—after all, if that is overdone, Ham is immediately the rube of the year in rock circles and his career could be set back to the point that he's again a local promo man. And he knows that.

" 'I can't afford to make mistakes,' Ham says flatly. 'If you have an act as big as ZZ Top, you *better* make the right moves.' "

The *New York Times*, lured perhaps by P.R. people stating the Texas tour would reach more people and make more money than any tour in history, including the Rolling Stones, reviewed the show in Atlanta. Easterners, adults, and rock critics still might not have liked the band, but they could no longer ignore them. Wayne King's *Times* feature concluded with the remarks of one concert-goer who wasn't interested in elaborate

analyses of ZZ Top's blues roots or Southern origins. A horde of past, present and probably future ZZ fans would undoubtably agree with her critical assessment: "It's fanny-shaking music."

Whether the tour broke attendance records, and whether it ended in the red (as Frank recently said) or made $11.5 million (as Lester Bangs reported in a 1980 *Musician* article), as soon as this large dose of Texana was over, the band dropped out of sight.

ZZ Top took Texas to the people and then the band disappeared from the scene in 1976.

CHAPTER 10

THE LONG VACATION

WHAT really happened between the end of the Texas tour in 1976 and the recording of *Deguello* in 1979? What were the real reasons for a layoff that lasted nearly three years? The band, and the people who knew them, have as many answers as there are thorns on a prickly cactus.

After the incessant touring of their first six years, the band undoubtedly needed some rest and recreation. The road had gotten to them. Had they continued touring night after night, city after city, they all feel they would have come to some bitter end, if not a permanent break-up. But a three-year vacation?

When they did return with *Deguello*, they had severed their connection with London and signed with Warner. Some think the long layoff was Ham's way of extricating ZZ from its London contract. Others think the band's deal with Ham was up.

A long-time Houston associate asks the obvious question: "If they were still signed with Ham, don't you think he would have them out working every night?"

It's been rumored that the band had Bill Ham audited. They thought they were making more money than they were actually getting. It had been a sticking point in the past. It was strange that the layoff involved such abstinence from all other musical activities. The band didn't play together; they made no public appearances with any other band of note, and they steered clear of the studio.

Billy loves to drop in on old friends and assorted club musicians and sit in for a song, if not a set. It's hard to believe he could have been prevented from jamming. He says he toured Europe with an avant-garde multimedia troupe (he also has some strange tales about chasing women to Tibet). It may have all been part of a Ham plan to make London think the band was breaking up and not to press for another record. On the other hand, according to the Dailys, London didn't have much of an investment in the band.

Ham wanted $1 million from Warner to sign the band. Although there were serious legal and business matters to be resolved before the band could tour and record again, the low profile may have fit in with Ham's master plan of media manipulation. Who knows if that was out of the Colonel Parker playbook? For whatever reasons, the strategy was *make them wait*.

The rabbi wears Ray-Bans.

Whatever the state of their business affairs, their personal lives, especially Dusty's and Frank's, were a bit rocky.

People close to the trio often say that Frank and Dusty's jobs have been on the line since the beginning. Despite the image of the happy, productive threesome, it has really been the Gibbons and Ham show.

The nagging insecurity and constant tension would not be easy for anyone to handle. Dusty has often said that he simply fell into the limelight, that he'd be just as happy playing bars. But given the way he thrives in front of huge audiences and enjoys his celebrity (and diamond rings and the DeLorean he couldn't afford on a bar band's salary) it's difficult to imagine him adjusting to downward mobility.

Dusty has always been a loner. Even as a kid, he would go to his room and spend hours there. As the years with ZZ wore on, it seemed that he was using his solitude to eat. Despite the band's growing popularity, his creative contributions were diminishing and his personal life was falling apart. He doesn't point to the road as the reason for the breakup of his marriage. "It's hard to stay married if you sell insurance," he says. But the road didn't help.

Several people have said that, during the band's lay-off, Dusty was sent to a fat farm in Mexico. Perhaps that gives a slightly different twist to the "vacation story" he told Jean-Charles Costa in *Record* magazine in 1983. Costa reported that Hill "lost himself in one of the Mexican villages he likes to go to when things get too heavy." Others say Dusty was merely threatened with deportation, that it became a frequently heard band joke. "Oh, can't find Dusty? He's making himself scarce because he's afraid Ham's going to send him to the fat farm."

The fat farm business may have been a joke. Frank recognized that his problems were serious. He's pretty clear about what he did during his time off: he got straight. He's proud of that and he has a right to be. There isn't anyone who has experienced a similar hell or who knew Frank in his previous incarnation as what he calls "a black belt in all drugs" who doesn't marvel at the way he turned his life around. The drugs and alcohol that seemed like exciting "wild things when he was fifteen" were making him a sick, tired and very unhappy man.

"I was irresponsible and self-centered, like all young self-serving dope fiends," he said, in Houston. "It was me first and to hell with the rest of it. I am just now on my first good dog. I had dogs when I was a dope fiend. I'd forget about em for a week, then go out back, dump a 35-pound sack of Alpo, forget about them for two weeks. I was not able to take care of even a *dog*." Beard's drug use wasn't the occasional Quaalude or the bit of grass in his sock. In his search for wilder things, Beard was using heroin as well as equally harmful quantities of pills and alcohol.

"The heroin would be serious," he says, "only to the extent that when I was in Houston, I was able to maintain a habit. When you're on the road, you cannot maintain a habit because you can't carry enough. I don't think the playing suffered that badly, but the sleep did."

His withdrawal involved less

Dusty Hill wonders why his right hand weighs 300 lbs. It's the Texas state seal on his pinky ring.

dope and more drink. Despite Beard's contention that "I never lost my primary talent, just all my secondary talents. Like being able to brush my teeth," there's been a noticable improvement in his drumming since he got straight. Frank's personal image is sharper—he's discovered Italian-designed clothes—and his playing is crisper and tighter now as well.

Beard went straight through a relationship with Bob Meehan, who runs the Palmer Drug Abuse Program in Houston. He later repaid the debt by becoming involved with the Program. It was his way, he explains, "of giving something back." He sponsored Carol Burnett's teenaged daughter, Carrie Hamilton, when she was involved in the program.

Frank's new bill of health convinced the woman who became his third wife, Debbie, to give him a second chance. She had been living in California, and also on her second divorce. (Her first marriage, curiously enough, was to the drummer in Neil Ford & the Fanatics.) Frank called her to say he'd gotten his act together and to ask, "Are you in love?" The result was what is, to date, ZZ's only happy couple. Frank, who describes himself as a "compulsive, excessive person" is now compulsively normal. Like Dusty, he gambles (he claims to beat Dusty, because Dusty gets drunk) but is devoted to golf. He won his country club's tournament. Although he zips around the course (his house overlooks it) in a customized black golf cart, he's won over those stodgier members of the club who objected to his presence.

Maybe they realize that Frank is now, as he describes himself, "no

different in his private life than a banker or a clothing store owner." He is, in fact, a clothing store owner. He and Debbie own an Italian sportsware boutique in a fancy

banker or a clothing store owner." He is, in fact, a clothing store owner. He and Debbie own an Italian sportsware boutique in a fancy suburban Houston mall. Although Beard got the Fila jogging suits ZZ wore on the *Eliminator* tour (the band's stage costumes were finally comfortable enough for him to play in), the other band members warn prospective customers about his store. The young millionaires conspiratorily whisper that Frank's goods are overpriced.

Frank wears headphones that feed him pre-recorded percussion tracks onstage.

CHAPTER 11

THE COMEBACK

BUT wherever the three ZZ's really were, whatever they did, and for whatever reasons, when they got back into the studio almost three years later, they were better.

During their time off, they'd grown beards. Even Frank Beard had one. He soon shaved it, to be different or obstinate or to prove that at least one member had a mug that wouldn't scare the little girls away from the record racks. It's possible that ZZ simply assumed they'd never win a sizable female audience. That seemed to be one part of the plan that Colonel Ham had neglected entirely, or given up on. Certainly Elvis, the Stones and the Beatles appealed, and catered to, girls as well as boys.

ZZ's material and attitude seemed directed at the beer drinkers and hell-raisers who'd been their constituency from the start. If there were some hard-living biker mamas, they could come along for the ride. But their boogie audience, like heavy metal audiences of the early 1970s, was predominantly male. While ZZ's lyrics have never been abusive, misogynist or blatantly offensive á la heavy metal, they've always had an undertone of

The trio ponders some new teen idol poses.

ZZ Top joins the army...

boys getting together and being silly about girls. They sound as if they're written during bull sessions of the he-man woman hater's club. It may not be surprising that they've never written any real love songs.

It's an attitude typified by his version of the cut that opens *Deguello*, a cover of "I Thank You," where Billy changes the "me's" of the verse to "it"—so that the lines read "You didn't have to hold it, you didn't have to squeeze it." Silly, perhaps inconsequential stuff, but it puts the material right in Tush country.

One wonders why ZZ chose to include two oldies (the other was "Dust My Broom") on a studio album, especially after they had so much time to perfect original material. It may have been a way to cover all of the bases. It was a time when soft rockers like Linda Ronstadt were having incredible suc-

cess with R&B re-makes, perhaps ZZ thought they'd have a hit with someone else's song on their Warner's debut. They might have: Billy's studio vocal performances were becoming really remarkable. And it's a performance, to be sure. A little bit of jive always sneaks around the corners of his phrasing, especially when he's doing one of his "black guy" imitations. Even though he groans, moans and hits notes effortlessly, the point is that this is entertainment, not some guy laying his guts on the line. The one problem with "I Thank You" isn't his vocal, which is surprisingly rich, or his guitar, which is wonderfully fluid, or the arrangement, which is quite inventive—it's the slightly mushy drumming. Frank lags behind, ever so slightly. But it's his only weak track on the album.

"Cheap Sunglasses" is far more representative of Frank's develop-

. . . and the Beach Boys.

ment as an original, tasteful drummer. The tricky, Billy Cobham-like roll he introduces at selective moments not only colors and heightens the dynamic tension of the track, it's a neat, classy lick.

Deguello has its share of filler, like "Lowdown in the Street," where Billy reels off a list of friends, accompanied by some great background vocals from Dusty and "Hi-Fi Mama" (Dusty does Little Richard again, to Chuck Berry-style lyrics) but it has more filler than previous records. *Deguello* had at least two songs worth the wait, proving that the band's vacation had not been in vain.

The blues and humor that made the band unique were fully integrated in "I'm Bad, I'm Nationwide." The title sounds like the ZZ power-chants of the early days. The chants were private jokes about a mythical ZZ Top character. Some of them read: "ZZ Top—he like a cold-blooded ice pack. He sits right on your head." "ZZ Top—like a fine plate of barbecue. Bear down on the meat and ease off the potato salad." "ZZ Top is like a beast on TNT, he stay in the groove." "ZZ Top, like a black on black Mark V—ain't a damn thing wrong with that, y'all." Billy finally managed to expand a chant into a full-length song that worked, and the nation got the joke. He also did it on "Cheap Sunglasses," which is not only one of the funniest songs ZZ Top ever recorded, but one of their most progressive. It sounds like Steely Dan meeting Frank Zappa. Both Dusty and Frank were influenced by early Zappa. As the American Blues they used to perform the entire *Freakout* album. (Although, as Dusty told *Rolling Stone*'s Kurt Loder, they all had "to

be on acid to do it right.") No credit is given for keyboards, so one assumes it's Billy playing Fender Rhodes behind the jazz-flavored guitar chords. There are some tricky time changes and a few subtle sound effects. Billy finally learned how to integrate the lessons of psychedelia without sounding slavishly derivative. He contributes some wonderful, perfectly timed flourishes. Although he didn't feel his extracurricular habits affected his playing, he sounds like a completely different, improved, drummer.

"Manic Mechanic" is a strange and interesting experiment with different, more progressive meters. Billy plays funky little licks over car noises. The vocal harks back to the psychedelic days with its altered, processed tone and the nonsense lyrics take the song out even further. "Manic Mechanic" might have been better as an instrumental, but the bizarre vocal track provides a peek into the deeper recesses of Gibbons' brain. It's one of the rare times his out-there studio experiments actually made it on to a ZZ record.

Gibbons sometimes makes up a tale about "Manic Mechanic" saying it's about a seven-foot auto racer he once knew who crashed and burned. But that's not the story told in the song.

There really isn't a story, that's the problem. It gives Billy a chance to do the routines, accents and characters he had been working on for years. This time, his "old blues guy" goes a little too far. He rasps at the end of the song: "Have mercy, Miss Percy, I done put the coon to it this time." The vocoder processing on the voice probably inspired this fooling around. Billy

"ZZ Top like a beast on TNT. He stay in the groove."

"ZZ Top like a cold-blooded ice pack. He sits right on your head."

"She loves my automobile."
Malibu, 1983.

Gibbons is an inveterate gadget-lover. He couldn't wait to use this new studio effect, even if he lacked the appropriate song or lyric.

But not only were Billy's characters getting out of hand in the studio, over the years he would sometimes become these creatures in real life. He walked around for days imitating the barbecue stand habitués, and it seemed to old friends that he no longer knew when to stop. He would call himself the Reverend Willy G., and adopt a down-home accent to match. He's taped radio shows pretending to be an evangelist. Later, he made serious inquiries about having "prayer balls" made up—little rubber balls stamped with prayers the evangelist Willy G. could market. It would enable the penitent to bounce and pray at the same time. He also handed out odd commercials, complete with female background vocals (possibly his voice at a different tape speed) advertising a nonexistent barbecue stand called "Queen Bee." He says they're done by a disc jockey friend, but the voice gushing over the good-ribs-and-hot-sauce sounds suspiciously like the mechanic who's put the coon to Miss Percy.

There was also another strange presence on *Deguello*, horns. The band members have frequently said that they decided something was missing on a few tunes and a horn section was just what the doctor ordered. They claim they added the horns behind producer Ham's back and that they sounded so good he had to leave them on "Hi-Fi Mama" and "She Loves My Automobile." One reason he might have objected was that Beard (alto), Hill (tenor) and Gibbons (baritone) played the saxophone themselves. Gibbons told Kurt Linhof they each

took one lesson. Given the barely-in-tune honking, the one-lesson story is entirely plausible. It's surprising that Ham wasn't there for the recording.

It sounds as if on most tracks, it was Dusty and Frank who weren't there. After the rhythm tracks were completed, Billy spent hours putting on his guitars and vocals—a process they were, by this time, excluded from. But Ham may have been less involved, even though *Deguello* was an important album for the band. It was their first Warner release. They were eager to prove that they'd been short-changed by London's lack of faith and promotion. The horns gave them an excuse to try another crazy idea on the road—even if it was a notch below hydraulically propelled buffalo. When the band toured in support of *Deguello*, they brought along a synchronized film clip and huge movie screen that allowed them to play onstage and accompany themselves as the Lone Wolf Horns, as well.

Robert Christgau, the "Dean of Rock Critics," had never been a ZZ fan. Yet even he surrendered to *Deguello*, giving it a not easily earned A- in his *Consumer Guide*, and this take: "These guys got off the road for real—sounds as if they spent all three years playing the blues on their front porch. The strident arena technique is gone, every song gives back a verbal phrase or two to make up for the musical ones it appropriates, and to vary the trio format they not only learned how to play horns but figured out where to put them. I've heard a shitload of white blues albums in the wake of Belushi and Aykroyd. This is the best by miles."

CHAPTER 12

EL LOCO

WITH *El Loco*, ZZ Top swung into the 80's in high spirits—literally and figuratively. The cover of their eighth album might have been mistaken for a *High Times* centerfold. The band posed with what-me-worry expressions and huge bags of marijuana, caught in the act by a sour-pussed border patrolman. Maybe this is how they thought their hellraising fans imagined them. And perhaps at this point in their careers, they figured that the only way they would sell was by appealing to the Cheech and Chong crowd. One wonders, though, how Frank, whose struggle with drugs was so painful could rationalize posing as a smuggler.

The songs on *El Loco* are partly prompted by the humor that inspired the cover. "Tube Snake Boogie" and "Ten Foot Pole" come from the he-man school of lyrics. So does "Pearl Necklace," one of ZZ's loveliest melodies. It suddenly switches gears to turn into one of their best hard rockers, and is complemented by some of Dusty's grittiest, live-sounding backups. Only the naive will think it's a sweet, romantic ditty about a guy and a girl en route to Tiffany's. "Pearl Necklace" is a popular

Power Summit: Dusty and Frank follow the leader.

The Reverend Willy G. and disciples convert the non-believers.

Southwestern expression for blowjob.

If the humor on *El Loco* is low-brow, the sound is state of the art. All of *El Loco* sounds great and sharp, the result, perhaps, of Bob Ludwig's excellent mastering. More pre-production time, better understanding of studio technology and the years on the road playing together make the band sound both looser and tighter. Billy is experimenting with different kinds of guitar sounds and solos from the National Steel work of "I Wanna Drive You Home" (another fusion of Gibbons' rock'n'roll and four-wheel-drive passions) to the cultured strands of wrenching electric lead he waves into "Pearl Necklace."

But the album reflected the band's desperation—they threw nearly every possible style against the wall in a see-what-sticks effort to come up with a hit. The band often says "Leila" was their first and last ballad. But "Esther Be the One", on *Deguello*, was a pretty slow number. Billy has frequently commented that "Leila" was ZZ's chance to meet the Beach Boys once in their careers. Unfortunately, they blew it. It's even more dismal than "Esther." Instead of being the band's potential MOR hit, it was one of the few tracks since their long vacation that sounded perfunctory. The bass part is unusually plodding. Billy sounds uncomfortable singing in the key. Or maybe he's incapable of whispering sweet nothings. He's such a superb mimic, though, it's hard to figure out why he couldn't do a better, cheekier, or funnier Brian Wilson voice.

There's an odd rumor about the track, too. A former employee of the band remembers a steel guitarist, possibly Mark Erlewine, who built many guitars for Billy until, (like many who've served Gibbons over the years, they had a falling out) rehearsing the pedal steel in Houston before joining the band in Memphis' Ardent Studios. Since no one but the engineers, Bill Ham and the band (and possibly their equipment roadies) are allowed in the studio when ZZ records, it's difficult to confirm who played on "Leila," or on any other cut. Part of the band's myth has not only been based on their self-penned material, but in creating every sound heard on their records or in concert.

It has often seemed amazing that only three people can create such a tremendous, heavily layered sound. It's no wonder: By *El Loco*, they had become more technologically sophisticated not only in the studio but on stage, too. They had learned that using prerecorded tapes in concert was the only way three people could make such a sound (and duplicate the many studio overdubs). Of course, many bands do this these days. But the band has come a long way from the early characterization as a natural, little old boogie trio.

On *El Loco*, Billy went overboard with some of the studio gimmicks. "Heaven, Hell or Houston" and "Ten Foot Pole" both feature similar bizarre plots and overly processed harmonizer vocals. The machines make Dusty's voice sound distant, as if he's singing through a broken megaphone in a wind tunnel. It's a shame to trick his great shouter's voice the way engineers are often forced to do with performers of lesser natural ability.

"Heaven, Hell or Houston" is a nod to Clapton's "In the Presence of the Lord" (and did Billy think nobody would recognize the resemblance of "It's So Hard" to a great R&B standard like "Cry to Me"?). He has claimed that "Ten Foot Pole" is about an incident that happened on his travels in the Himalayas. Somehow, the song doesn't back that up, and the story sounds suspiciously like his elaborate tale on the origins of "Master of Sparks." You don't need a tale if you have a song, and *El Loco* has a couple great rockers like the juvenile "Tube Snake Boogie" and "Pearl Necklace."

But for the most part the band seemed confused. "Groovy Little Hippie Pad" and "Party on the Patio" (two throwaways—perhaps a few other blues covers might have been preferable) seem to be concessions to the new wave scene they couldn't ignore. As they were becoming bad and nationwide (if not yet bad and international) they weren't sure how to break out of a strict blues and boogie form. Their ability to handle this transition would determine their fate. ZZ Top was on the verge of becoming more successful than previous Southern bands.

They were even beginning to get some critical respect. The late great Lester Bangs, who admitted in his *Musician* piece that he had once been "an unbeliever too" was not alone in his newfound appreciation of what he described as ZZ's "friendly frenzy." Gibbons returned the favor by inviting Bangs for a weekend of Texas fun, namely hunting and fishing. Gibbons says he didn't know which Bangs (who despite his gonzo lifestyle was basically a city slicker) feared more: the firearms or the worms used for bait.

Despite critical acceptance and higher standards of living, ZZ Top still hadn't hit the jackpot. *El Loco* only went gold and the band wasn't quite sure how they fit into a record industry buffeted by change. As seasoned rock'n'rollers and rebels in their own right they identified with the spirit and attitude of a new generation of punks. Yet they were not quite sure how to retain their original essence and at the same time move into the future.

CHAPTER 13

THE BIG DADDY/ ELIMINATOR

BILLY Gibbons had ordered his car so long ago that everybody had forgotten about it. From time to time he'd call to check on how it was doing, but the damn thing was taking so long it seemed it might never get finished. "It" was the hot rod of his dreams, a 1934 Model T that he wanted customized and rebuilt. It was the kind of car he built in plastic in miniature as a kid. It had the kind of pin-striping that he had put on one of his early guitars. He realized such a dream mobile was possible when he'd gone to a car show sometime in 1975 and spied another customized beauty, the California Kid. That wasn't for sale, even though Billy finally had the cash for it. He couldn't find another, either, until Don Thelan came up with the 1934 Model T. Billy had some neat ideas for the car. Besides having it repainted and rebuilt, he wanted gold records in the wheels. But who would've thought that the whole project would take *years*?

The car was like any of the other custom-made things he was dreaming up and trying to track down (like brothel creepers for the band's videos) or build (like prayer balls or little travel guitars). When he was working on songs for what was to become the band's ninth and most successful album, he had another brainstorm. How about a machine that would make it sound as if he were calling long distance? That would make for some of his best jokes ever. Much better than some of the things he said he'd done recently—like stamping Dusty's name on 2,000 postcards in response to ads in biker magazines, resulting in so much mail that the mailman refused to deliver the two large bags arriving daily, or announcing a former girlfriend's name on a radio station in the Grand Caymans, where he says she married a scuba diver—and giving free albums and posters to anyone who showed up at a ZZ concert in Florida with a British passport or tickets from the Grand Caymans; even better than writing to NASA trying to get ZZ booked as the first band on the space shuttle. Or trying to convince people he saw Howard Hughes lying in state.

When he started working on songs for the *El Loco* follow-up, it seemed like he was spending as much time checking on the progress of his long-distance-call machine as he was thinking up guitar licks. The problem was that

The Big Daddy takes a dip. Malibu, 1983.

the guy who was building it wanted too much money. Gibbons, for all we know, still isn't able to call people from Houston and make them believe he's in Rome. But the car was finally ready. Even though it didn't have gold records in the wheels, with its new Chevy engine, gorgeous red paint job, and mean-looking chassis, the hot rod was something else.

Bill Ham no sooner saw it than he convinced Billy his new toy was too good for his personal use. It ought to be used, somehow, for the band. Maybe it had something to do with figuring a way to write off the high cost of the vehicle. At $50,000 (maybe more) it was no go-cart.

The car could solve one problem that had been bothering them lately. They were afraid they were starting to show their age. They covered their faces with beards and their balding heads with hats; sunglasses (cheap or expensive)

usually did the trick for crow's feet. But they still wanted their next album to be a killer, and no one was going to buy it because they were sex symbols or teen idols. Using the car as a symbol could be the perfect solution.

Their fans might identify with the car. ZZ started going to drag races to find out what the crowd was into—and the male fans were basically the same group that always responded to the band. There was also a possibility the band might provide the soundtrack to a film (or so Gibbons told *Rolling Stone's* Kurt Loder) about drag racing. Someone involved with the project suggested they name the car "Top Fuel." But Billy's baby wasn't a high-performance car; she was a hot rod. They settled on the term used for the winner of the final heat, Top Eliminator. Then it was shortened, for convenience, to Eliminator.

A righteous pair of headlights.

Their moment, they were sure, had arrived. They were going to be bad and global. They were going to put more of themselves and their time into the songs, the production and the show. They were going to give it their all. The machine was primed, ready to roar and they were ready to floor it.

Frank had a studio in his house overlooking the Quail Valley golf course. It made rehearsing and preproduction a lot easier. Frank liked to go in there and bash around occasionally, but he mostly practiced golf strokes. What was he going to practice, anyway—drum solos? The only time ZZ Top ever had drum solos was in the very early days when they didn't have enough material to fill a set. Drum solos bored Frank to tears. In fact, the finest drum solo he'd ever heard came from raindrops beating on an old air cooler. He'd lain there once and listened to that for hours.

No one knew how to operate that studio except the guy who built it. That caused some real laughs. Bill Ham showed up at rehearsal and told the studio wizard, Linden Hudson, who'd built the place while house-sitting for Frank that his services weren't needed, he could leave. So he left. Bill Ham didn't know which switch turned on the mikes or whatever. After a bit of this fooling around Frank went to play golf, which is really what he preferred to do on his rare fine days at home. Dusty drove off in his DeLorean. Billy sat there and fiddled. Somebody had to come up with the songs.

Hudson knew his way around a studio, having worked in a few of them around the country. He also wrote songs. He'd sung with a local outfit, the Van Wilk band. And

he'd been a DJ (called himself Jack Smack back then) on KROL, a Houston station. He thought he knew what it took to put together a good rock song, but so far he hadn't had much luck on his own. But then again, not everybody gets the breaks. He thought, after 15 yers of trying, that he'd finally gotten his. He knew Billy back in his Jack Smack days, when Billy was frantic to buddy up with any DJ who would play ZZ's records, and they'd run around some. They'd lost touch over the years, but ZZ was hardly ever in Houston with all that touring. The band had been away so long, maybe they didn't even consider it home anymore. That really got to plenty of people in town.

As for Linden, he'd never known Frank too well until the drummer contacted him. He'd been suggested as an engineer for a benefit album Frank was producing for the Palmer Drug Rehabilitation folks. They got on so well that Frank asked him to live at his house. He could look after it while Frank was away, and help ZZ out. Linden never bothered to ask for a salary or a contract. He was being invited to join the family. It was just the break he'd been waiting for.

He didn't even charge for building the studio, or installing a burglar alarm or feeding the dog. He did complain when Frank would come off the road and scream that the lawn hadn't been mowed. Frank's best friend was a shrink who played golf with him. Sometimes the situation got so bad that Linden went and talked to him, too. Frank's friend explained that the road created some pretty strange conditions. The members of the band were treated like kings. It

was only natural that they'd come back and act snobby for a while.

Dusty didn't like what happened to him on the road, either. He woke up in his own bed in Houston and dialed room service. He sometimes found himself acting out an ugly scene from a movie. The band would tease him about his fondness for movies. He'd watch anything. One film stood out in his mind. Kirk Douglas was in it, playing a general. Susan Hayward was in it, too. There was a scene where the general rushed out a door, and Susan Hayward and everyone says, "Jeez, what a jerk." Sometimes, Dusty went on a date or out with friends, and would go through a door first, and jump into the limo before the ladies, because that was tour protocol. Then catch himself.

"Jeez, what a jerk," they'd probably say. It really bothered him.

The only person who didn't seem disturbed by the transition between road and home was Billy. For one thing, he didn't really have a home. He had a $500,000 townhouse which was sort of a one room/duplex affair—not really much space. (The location, not far from his mother in Tanglewood, overlooking a muddy little river, the Buffalo Bayou, makes it so expensive.) But there's not much in the town house besides a couch and a jukebox full of George Jones, Roky Ericson and a tune called "Freeze a Yankee" (accompanied by his scribbled note "I don't know who done it, but it's good!"). Billy often joked, "I don't go to bed, I go to couch." It's often easier for him

Does Kirk Douglas do this, too? Dusty swings low as ZZ's moment arrives, 1983.

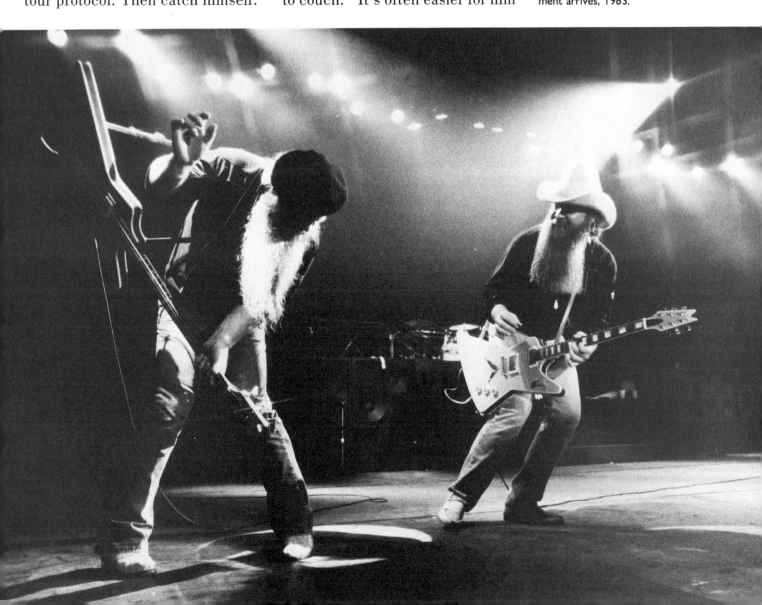

to check into a hotel around the corner. There's room service, or someone to pay to smuggle in a bottle or six-pack after hours, and people to take messages. He never has to feel as if he's not on the road, the center-stage attraction in his permanent three-ring show. Frank can't understand it. He offered his decorator's services to Billy. She came back shaking her head, after months of trying to order the man some furniture so he wouldn't have to "go to couch." She said she couldn't work with him. He was impossible, he didn't know what he wanted. But maybe he does know what he wants. He wants the show never to stop.

The show is a *lot* of fun. Billy has a knack for making sure whoever

he takes along for the ride is there, center stage, along with him. As a man who's known him long enough not to be seduced into going along says: "Billy has a genuine talent for making it seem he is your best friend in the world at that particular moment."

It is a useful talent in his line of work. It comes in handy when confronting an audience or, on a more intimate scale, when conducting an interview. Writers have a wonderful time with Billy Gibbons. He'll take them fishing and hunting or to Las Vegas or New Orleans.

Sometimes he'll do something funny, to his friends. Once he sent two tickets to someone in Houston for a ZZ Top show in Germany with a "Wish you were here" invitation.

Then he neglected to send the plane tickets that would enable them to get to Germany.

Nearly everyone who's known him has had the experience of being asked for a favor by Billy. It will usually go like this: he'll want them to drive him somewhere, to look at a guitar or a car, say, and he'll promise to buy them a barbecue. The poor chump will do whatever errand or task is asked. In the end, he'll end up buying his own barbecue and Billy's as well.

Linden Hudson didn't mind paying for his own spareribs but he wasn't credited for his contribution to *El Loco*, when ZZ Top used the recording he had engineered of "Groovy Little Hippie Pad" because the Memphis version wasn't as good as the demo cut in Frank Beard's home studio. He took Billy's word that they hadn't been able to get his name to the printer's on time. It seemed a bit strange, given that Gibbons had plenty of time to check and approve anything so important as cover art and credits. After all, Hudson was part of the family. It was a mistake. It wouldn't happen again.

Because Linden was part of the family, he wanted the band to do well. He knew how badly they wanted this next album to go plati-

ZZ had to improvise when their costumes and equipment were stolen at the start of the *Eliminator* tour, 1983.

num, so he didn't mind sharing the results of his computer study with Billy. Linden was always doing computer studies. It was something that fascinated him, like studio technology. He thought he might understand the components of popular songs better if he fed certain data into his computer. It might help him understand what hits of any given period share. He first found out about speed; all the songs he studied deviated no more than one beat from 120 beats per minute.

Billy immediately started to write some songs with 120 beats per minute. Linden helped out with a couple, like "Under Pressure" and "Sharp Dressed Man." Someone had to help Billy out. Dusty and Frank didn't even like to rehearse much. Their studio absence wasn't really a problem though. The bass and drum parts were easily played with a synthesizer or Linn drum machine. The machines could be programmed to play styles more modern than Dusty's or Frank's. Frank often jokes that he only knows three beats: the shuffle, the cut shuffle, and the monkey beat. He has a few names for some of his standard licks, like "the workhorse." The Linn was a little more versatile and realistic. Its perfection was the only way you could tell it wasn't a human drummer. Bill Ham couldn't tell. He came to rehearsal a couple of days after Linden and Billy had finished putting "Under Pressure" together. They'd been so jazzed about the song, that they were still working on it one night when Frank and Debbie were getting ready to go to bed. Frank stuck his head round the door and asked Billy and Linden to keep it quiet.

Anyway, Bill Ham was crazy jazzed about the song. He came down to rehearsal and asked the band to run through that great new tune Billy had played him a tape of. "What tune?" Dusty and Frank wanted to know. "You know, that tune you wrote the other day, 'Under Pressure,'" Ham insisted. Finally Dusty threw his hands in the air with an "I-give-up look on his face. Ham, exasperated, went on to something else.

Linden didn't foresee the song-credit omissions when he helped Billy write "Under Pressure," "Sharp Dressed Man" or several other *Eliminator* songs he says he worked on. Like every other musician who jammed with Billy and later paid for it, he wasn't about to insist on a signed agreement before picking up a pen or an instrument.

Linden is a talented musician whose tricky synthesizer-based music sounds like a Texas Thomas Dolby. But Billy Gibbons' powerful, inimitable presence is stamped on those ZZ Top songs. Linden is currently signed with legendary producer Huey Meaux. His songs have a great deal of promise, but he's not yet the singer or interpreter Billy is. It's difficult, therefore, to determine how much Hudson contributed to the songs he claims he co-wrote with Gibbons.

"Thug" is another, more clear-cut case. Hudson wrote it and copyrighted it. He played it for Billy, who said he wanted to buy it and produce it for his girlfriend at the time. She was a singer named Diane Taylor, the Blues Wailer. Eventually, ZZ Top decided to use the song on *Eliminator*. They and Bill Ham refused to discuss the question of royalties or album points with him. They didn't deny

Sharp Dressed Men bask in front of their precious metals.

he wrote the song. They claim they bought it from him. Hudson says the $750 check he received was not payment for the song, but for engineering services performed for the band. The question remains: how could he have sold the song without any accompanying paperwork or transfer of copyright?

Yet for all the ugliness behind the scenes, *Eliminator* was still one of the great rock records of 1983. It is the best, most fun, most cohesive and fully realized album that ZZ Top had made to date. As 1984 came to a close, it was still Warner's best-selling, unstoppable album.

The eight-month *Eliminator* tour sold out arenas across the country and in Europe (where ZZ isn't as well established. They've only toured there three times).

There was a new crowd at the shows, a striking contrast to the familiar boozing, hulking bikers. The *Eliminator* audiences were wholesome MTV-watching teens. No one was more surprised than the band as they looked from the stage to see so many fresh-faced young girls (approximately 50% of the crowd) bopping to "Gimme All Your Lovin' " and "Sharp Dressed Man."

Nor was the crowd dancing in vain. ZZ Top may be one of the few arena bands that actually gives its audience reason to bop. The last night of the *Eliminator* tour in Biloxi, in February 1984 (also the band's 14th anniversary) was a real onstage fiesta—but so were all the other dates on the tour. No matter what they may do offstage, it's hard to believe this band has ever failed

its audience where it counts—on the gig. They don't seem to know the meaning of a "bad night."

Eliminator audiences were greeted by a monster blowup of the car, complete with glowing headlights. (The real hot rod went on its own car show tour, and although Billy and the band coasted briefly in it durng the video shots, Billy has yet to drive his dream mobile.) But once the band kicked into their past and present hits (from "Tush" to "Gimme Some Lovin' ") the car wasn't necessary. Even if they were being assisted by tape effects, and crazy effects (like maracas dangling from the ceiling to shake for "Party on the Patio"), the music and the mood was terrific.

Given the exciting pace, one wonders why they ever needed the buffalo and steer. Their full-tilt boogie, even with tape assistance, is basically the roar of three guys. It's a stampede in its own right. Dusty and Billy duckwalk, shimmy and shake non-stop (incredibly gracefully, considering their waistlines were approaching buffalo-belt size on the last tour). They say they make up their unique dance steps on the spot. But if something works, they try to remember to use it again. Even though they rarely socialize offstage, in concert Billy and Dusty relay loads of information to each other. They're not talking about cues to the next move, or changes in the set list. They're talking about the fans in the front rows. Dusty confesses, "I might ask Billy if he's seen the girl in the front or ask: 'What's with that big guy over there, is he on quays or what?' "

Eliminator audiences were also treated to a state-of-the-art laser show that enhanced spacier selections like "Manic Mechanic." As the absurd vocal rumbled out of the offstage tape deck, Billy and Dusty wandered about the massive flight deck-sized stage, bounded by stripes of green light, as if they were prisoners on some strange galaxy.

Many contemporary groups must rely on lighting tricks, smoke bombs and other stage gimmickry because their music or stage performance can't sustain 90 minutes' interest. In ZZ Top's case, the effects are only extra cheese on the enchilada. Few bands have two lead vocalists as powerful or as fun as Dusty Hill and Billy Gibbons. The interaction between them, as they trade vocals that Billy often handles alone on the records, is really special. Frank, although he's playing along with a click track or other taped effects, has a distinctly punchy and steady attack.

As the virtuoso of the trio, Billy is the only one who solos. As Frank and Dusty put it, the only time they had to solo was in the early days, when they had to pad a skimpy set. Perhaps one of the reasons this combination works so well, especially live, is that they know their strengths. As a rhythm section holding down the bottom beneath Gibbons' soulful flights, there are no better men for the job. As for Gibbons' playing, he manages to pull off an entire evening's worth of noteworthy leads without ever relying on sheer noise or frenzied flash.

There are almost no other world-class guitar heroes who can turn the show into a nutty professor's revival meeting, as Billy does on "Fool For Your Stockings." When ZZ ended their *Eliminator* shows

with a classic spoof: smokebomb, scenery collapsing and a dummy "Roadie" falling from a lighting scaffold (which spared them the nuisance of an encore), it was hard not to be moved. Perhaps not moved to tears, but certainly to laughter. Even without an encore, the audiences on this tour didn't feel cheated. Few big-time bands give their fans so much in entertainment and music. The new album and shows, plus their great videos, were all solid.

ELIMINATOR — The Clips

Each time a new video was released, the album jumped back into the top part of the charts. As of Dec. 1984, *Eliminator* had been on the charts ninety weeks, and showed no sign of stalling. Even "TV Dinners," a clumsy animation done by the new video department at Ardent Studios in Memphis boosted sales. Despite the heavy-handed direction and computer graphic cliches, kids loved the ge-

Hot-rodding prisoners on some strange galaxy: Dusty and Billy, 1983

nuinely funny song that showed the band capable of more than Tush-y jokes. Without a video, "TV Dinners " with its wonderful images of blue frozen turkey and icy stabs of rinky-dink organ might have remained stuck in the deep freeze with the rest of the album's filler.

As Dusty explained during the band's stop in Des Moines, the band accepts that some of an album's songs are going to be weaker than others. They didn't have great expectations for "Legs," which was surprisingly elevated to hit single status (the most successful of all *Eliminator's* singles, in fact) thanks to another sexy girls and car fast-paced Tim Newman clip.

The success of the band's video clips is all the more remarkable considering that Colonel Ham never wanted ZZ Top to appear on television in the first place. Somehow, he thought, it would destroy their mystique. Before MTV, he had turned down all offers for their appearance on rock shows like *The Midnight Special* or variety shows like *Saturday Night Live. Saturday Night* featured them anyway—but as presidential write-in candidates, not musical guests. After Father Guido Sarducci "nominiated" the band on the air in Jan. 1984, the band actually received 131,384 votes on the special phone lines set up for the stunt. Gibbons promptly jumped into the campaign, promising, if elected, a "hot guitar on every table." To this date, ZZ never appeared live on American TV. On the MTV awards broadcast from Radio City in Sept. 1984, they brought the car and the girls, but no microphones or instrument cords. Despite their unspectacular performance, they still cop-

A Hard Day's Night. What would have happened if ZZ Top had waited for Ham's movie?

ped (and deserved) awards for best group. And Tim Newman walked away with an equally hard-earned trophy for Best Director.

What was it about those first two videos that captured hearts and imaginations in the first place? But most viewers loved the rock'n'roll fantasy the clips presented. In both early shorts, the band's handed over the keys to the car and presumably the three beauties who drove it to an ordinary guy. The band was in the background, appearing as benevolent, smiling uncles. The scenes were shot from the viewpoint of the ordinary guy, presumably the viewer. Here, the band seemed to suggest as they dangled their sparkling keychains, is the power of rock'n'roll. Here is the magic that will set you free.

In a sense, when it came to the video business, the band were even greater rubes than the garage attendant in the first clip. Dusty recalled shooting a scene where the actor playing the beneficiary of the band's largess went into a footloose frenzy in front of the band-stand.

'Shoot!" exclaimed Dusty, interrupting the band's lip-sync'ed version of their hit. "That's good!"

"Cut!" screamed the director, as everyone silently cursed Hill (who didn't know their "garage attendant" had serious dance training) for making them suffer through another take.

Bill Ham wasn't quite as enthusiastic as the judges and the public were about Newman's work. Newman felt "Legs" would be his last association with the group. What was interesting about the "Legs" video was the way it assumed the viewer was familiar

with the characters and scenario from previous clips. As with "Sharp Dressed Man" and "Gimme All Your Lovin' " three gorgeous girls appeared in the *Eliminator* hot rod to rescue a hapless hero—or in this case, heroine. Ham was disturbed because Newman placed the action in a shopping mall, which was not in his estimation a classy enough location for his boys. According to Newman, Ham kept threatening to pull the plug on "Legs" until it went on the air. But although the direction, dialogue and plot were sophisticated by rock-video standards, the band's antics, which had seemed so fresh and off-the-cuff in "Sharp Dressed Man" and "Gimme," were becoming pat.

Ham showed up on the sets dressed in his idea of a Hollywood director's outfit, a safari suit. Observers noted he seemed uncomfortable with the band's appearance in a situation he couldn't control. As it is, ZZ Top appeared only once on live television in Germany. They only did so because it was deemed essential for their careers on the Continent. Ham would rather have saved the band, or so Tim Newman felt, for *his* movie. After all, remember Elvis and the Colonel. Hollywood is the way they went.

ELIMINATOR—The Cuts

But the videos would just be pretty, catchy images without the songs that anchor them.

From the opening crack of "Gimme All Your Lovin' " *Eliminator* simply sounded hotter than anything ZZ Top had done before. The songs, with a few exceptions ("Bad Girl," "If I Could Only Flag Her Down" and "Dirty Dog"), were meticulously crafted, loaded with hooks and primed to detonate on impact. Despite its deceptive three-chord-boogie simplicity, "Gimme All Your Lovin' " is fleshed out with crazy "Manic Mechanic" grunts that Billy finally learned to employ judiciously (as punctuation rather than as lead vocals). There are also ricocheting guitar effects and washes of synthesizer that become apparent after repeated hearings. After 15 years, the band, with help from Terry Manning, had learned how to use studio technology to layer and construct a seemingly spontaneous song. Despite Linden Hudson's claims, the band (or Billy) wrote and recorded "Gimme All Your Lovin' " in Memphis, without him. The feel and speed are similar to "Sharp Dressed Man," which employed Hudson's 120-beat-per-minute theory. The feel, the enthusiasm, the snappy beat and the crisp clean sound propelled *Eliminator* into the ears and hearts of 5 million people who previously could have cared less about the boogie band of *Rio Grande Mud*.

As for Billy's playing, no metronomic equation could get what the man gets from his hands and fingers. What he is getting is pretty amazing, even on the lamest tracks of *Eliminator*. He may be playing the same old licks, but he's never before put them together so smoothly. As he fires off the chunky rhythmic solos of "Gimme All Your Lovin' ," he finally fulfills the boasts and potential of his early Sidewalk days. Jimi would be proud. But Billy's learned to incorporate those early influences into a rich, soulful style he can hon-

estly claim as his own. Although he's been playing many of these blues-derived licks for years, and he borrows the Stones' image for the lyric, he does make good on "Gimme All Your Lovin'"'s threat: he whips it like a new boy should.

His singing has also undergone a similar evolution. His bluesy variations no longer sound as if they might have come from some Amos 'n'Andy routine.

On "Under Pressure" and "Sharp Dressed Man" he makes the plots funny and convincing. Even on "I Need You Tonight," his plaintive, raspy moan accomplishes what he has never before done on a slow, serious song, he sounds believable.

Of course, Gibbons is still more effective as a shuck-and-jivester than as a soldier of love. But whatever category "Under Pressure," "Sharp Dressed Man," "Gimme Some" et al, fall into, they're some of his best work. The sad thing is that ZZ has grown far away from the band described on the first album. Those liner notes cannot

help but serve as an ironic fillip today. They no longer play their "blues rock openly, honestly and spontaneously." Rather, they've come closer to what the note's author (Ham?) protested so vehemently: "homogenized rock, synthesized music, retakes, overdubbing, multi multi-tracking."

Although they are still one of the great, entertaining arena attractions, more and more the sounds of their recent records are reproduced by tapes that accompany the performance. Frank Beard now wears headphones during concerts. He's playing along with a click track and with recordings of drum machines and percussion effects.

Drum machines, multi-tracking and synthesizers, and all, *Eliminator* was ZZ Top's first Grammy Award nomination. Up against the Police, the band felt they had no chance to win, and didn't bother attending the ceremonies. "I hate to lose," explained Frank, the inveterate gamesman and gambler.

The transition from boogie band to rich businessmen has not been as easy as shifting a roadster into a higher gear. A photographer who did their recent publicity stills had to airbrush off the monstrous gold and diamond Rolexes the trio favors. They're no longer blues bums but middle-age men who own shopping malls and oil leases.

The band has long maintained an uneasy truce among themselves. They don't socialize off the road. On the road they often don't see each other until showtime, frequently traveling in separate limousines. But after 15 years they no longer have to spend every moment together. There is never any doubt, once they hit the stage, that

end of the *Eliminator* tour, "love to play." Maybe more frequent interaction would rob them of that spark they ignite on stage.

There have been rumors emanating from Houston that most of their longtime road crew, including the devoted Pete Tickle, who used to lug Billy's equipment around in a bread truck in the early Sidewalk days, have quit or been fired. And in August, 1984, two bookkeepers who had worked for the band's management company for several years were arrested on charges of embezzling at least $1 million from them.

More disturbing, perhaps, is what's happened to Billy Gibbons. Although there are those who say he hasn't changed since the days when he only *thought* he was a star, ZZ's current fame has had a sometimes frightening effect on the man. There are a few acquaintances who date the real change in his behavior to his father's death.

He only seems happy when at the center of constant commotion. Thanks to the power of video, his beard and costume make him as recognizable on the streets of America as a character from *Hollywood Squares*. Just in case anyone misses the beard, he usually wears a baseball hat that spells out his affiliation: ZZ Top. That makes him easy to spot, even when he's going incognito by tucking his beard in his collar or donning costumes to go with whatever identity he's chosen for the day.

The Reverend Willy G. wears a long frock coat, and carries a bottle of hot sauce. As The Sharp Dressed Man, he sports buttersoft Italian loafers, sheer socks he says he gets in "the Black part of town," an exquisitely-tailored blue pin-

Billy takes off his Rolex and whips it like a new boy should.

striped suit and a club print Ralph Lauren tie that would be acceptable on Wall Street. However, he neglects to remove the price tag ($37.50) from the tie. And he rarely forgets to stuff his pockets with ZZ Top souvenir keychains (which Tim Newman says he created for the videos—and gets no share of the profits from the sale of $10 chains) but he often forgets his wallet. Which explains why so many people who've been promised a barbecue in return for performing some simple favor often get stuck with the tab.

It doesn't bother Billy either, that the people he gives the keychains to frequently want

something else—a T-shirt, concert tickets, an 8-track or an album. The fans who often besiege him in restaurants and airports demanding autographs don't know his name. They address him generically, as "ZZ Top." One of the best lines came from a stewardess on a recent flight from New Orleans to Houston who asked him whether the ZZ Top on his hat was the name of his boat.

It's not a boat, but sometimes it seems to be turning into a monster. Gibbons' appearance at a Houston bar where Lanier Greig, with whom he formed ZZ Top so many years ago, was performing recently, was not atypical.

A waitress went up to Greig, who was on stage, to tell Lanier a friend

was there to see him. During the break between sets, Greig found Billy at a table, surrounded by drinking companions. When he tapped Billy on the shoulder and said hello, Billy asked him who he was.

"It's Lanier, Billy, Lanier." Billy started crying. He was, Greig said, fairly loaded, and had to be propped up by a member of his "crude crew" (as his gang of rich Houston pals are fond of describing themselves) who kept prodding him, "Hey, buddy, hey."

Billy brought up something he's talked about many times, but never followed through on. How would Lanier like to play keyboards on the next ZZ Top show or album? But he wanted to get out of the bar.

Why wouldn't Lanier come with him? Lanier couldn't explain to Gibbons that he couldn't leave, he was performing in the bar and had at least another set to do, but he'd be sure to come down and talk to him during the next break. He reminded Billy of the deal they'd made so many years ago, as they drove out to the barbecue stands and Gracie's chicken farm. Didn't Billy remember how they pledged whoever made it first in the music biz would help the other?

Of course, Billy remembered. "Why do you think I'm here?"

But at the next break, when Lanier came off the bandstand, Billy was gone.

More and more, his old friends say, Billy seems to be turning into a ZZ Top character, the person in all the wild stories, for real. What will become of a man like that? But more important, perhaps, what will become of the band? Now that they've achieved the bad and international reputation they were shooting for all along, what will they do with it? Will they be able to top the big daddy, *Eliminator*? Could anyone?

In order to maintain *Eliminator's* modern pace, ZZ may have to rely on technology that will make Frank and Dusty's contributions less significant in the studio. Live, there's no doubt, though, that the trio will continue to provide one of the most professional, hysterical and uplifting arena shows in the world for many tours to come. Maybe Ham's strategy was right all along. Given their past history—from buffalo to hot rods—it's anyone's guess as to what's coming.

One thing is certain: in a time-honored tradition of rock and roll, one misfit kid from Tanglewood was able to reinvent himself. And as so many who knew him then, and now have said about Billy Gibbons and his Svengali, Bill Ham, they not only took ZZ to the very Top. They created a legend. Have mercy.

No room for derringers in these sandals. As ZZ prepared its *Eliminator* follow-up, Dusty was injured in a bizarre accident. By Spring 1985, he was ready to rock again.

DISCOGRAPHY

First Album, London Records, 1970.
Rio Grande Mud, London Records, 1972.
Tres Hombres, London Records, 1973.
Fandango!, London Records, 1975.
Tejas, London Records, 1976.
Best of ZZ Top, London Records, 1977.
Deguello, Warner Bros., 1979.
El Loco, Warner Bros., 1981.
Eliminator, Warner Bros., 1983.

VIDEOGRAPHY

"Sharp Dressed Man" Directed by Tim Newman
"Gimme All Your Lovin' " Directed by Tim Newman
"Legs" Directed by Tim Newman
"TV Dinners" Directed by Maurious Pinzner

ABOUT THE AUTHOR

Deborah Frost has written for *Rolling Stone*, the *Village Voice*, *People*, the *Boston Phoenix* and many other magazines. She lives in New York City.

ABOUT THE PHOTOGRAPHER

Bob Alford has been shooting live performances of major recording artists throughout the U.S., Europe and Japan since 1970. He first photographed ZZ Top in 1974 and has produced the *El Loco* and *Eliminator* album covers as well as ZZ Top's tour books. He lives in Detroit.